"Eddie Gibbs has not only been a gift to the church for as long as I can remember but someone who has been hugely influential in my life and ministry. The beauty of Eddie's life is that he has always been a practitioner and a scholar, refusing to let the hallowed halls of academia change, in any way, the calling of his life as a disciple of Jesus. This poignant book of Eddie's reflections will illuminate what life can be like if you follow Jesus over the course of your life with steadfastness, vigor and adventure. I can't recommend it highly enough."

Mike Breen, founder and global team leader, 3DM

"From the air raid sirens of WWII in England through the era of iPad and Droid enthusiasm, Eddie Gibbs, the mechanic's son, who never had a library in his home as a youngster, shares his unique perspective on life's journey and lessons learned on both sides of the pond. From the time Eddie and I first met in 1982-1983 in preparation for the Mission England efforts throughout the United Kingdom, I have been learning from him. His insights are refreshing. This book is no different, as Eddie guides us through life committed to Christ, its struggles, hurdles, joys and growth. GibbsNext would have been a great title for this book, for Eddie has become a guru for all who know and appreciate that perspective of ministry in culture as well as practical and theological development."

Tom Phillips, vice president of crusades, Billy Graham Evangelistic Association

"Eddie Gibbs loves the church, and his heart aches when it falls short. With humility and humor, Eddie shares challenging words in this book, words that can only emerge out of a lifetime of service with those who are on the forefront of ministry so that the church might advance. Read this book slowly. It is full of wisdom from a seasoned pastor, missionary and professor who through the experiences of his life and his family reminds church leaders what is most essential for fruitful ministry. These are words to read and then to incorporate into our lives."

Kurt Fredrickson, associate dean for Doctor of Ministry and Continuing Education, assistant professor of pastoral ministry, Fuller Theological Seminary

"Sage advice, sound teaching, fascinating stories—such jewels you will find in Eddie Gibbs's new book, *The Journey of Ministry*, where he shares a lifetime of insight and experience. I had the privilege of sitting under his instruction at Fuller Theological Seminary; he is a master teacher. You may not agree with every conclusion he has reached over 50 years of ministry (and he has come with some amazing insights)—but you will be challenged, instructed and inspired by his life, ministry and vision for the kingdom. I know I was."

Jim Belcher, author of *Deep Church*

"Eddie is one of the few elder statesmen around in missional church circles. I am personally always thankful for Eddie and deeply value everything he has to say. In this reflective book, the sage offers sagely advice on issues ranging from ministry, spirituality, character and of course . . . mission. A worthy read."

Alan Hirsch, author, activist, dreamer (www.alanhirsch.org)

"Eddie Gibbs, a cherished mentor to me and thousands of others, is a national treasure in both the United States and the United Kingdom. Now I want to say more: the godly wisdom communicated in *The Journey of Ministry* deserves a global hearing."

Bishop Todd Hunter, founder, Churches for the Sake of Others (C4SO), author, *Christianity Beyond Belief*

"Pay attention to this book! Eddie Gibbs is weaving gold from the many threads of his life."

David Hansen, Kenwood Baptist Church, Cincinnati, Ohio, author of *The Art of Pastoring*

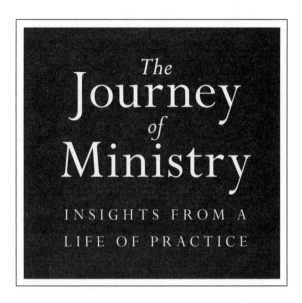

The
Journey
of
Ministry

INSIGHTS FROM A
LIFE OF PRACTICE

EDDIE GIBBS

Foreword by Richard Mouw

IVP Books

An imprint of InterVarsity Press
Downers Grove, Illinois

InterVarsity Press
P.O. Box 1400, Downers Grove, IL 60515-1426
World Wide Web: www.ivpress.com
E-mail: email@ivpress.com

InterVarsity Press® is the book-publishing division of InterVarsity Christian Fellowship/USA®, a movement of students and faculty active on campus at hundreds of universities, colleges and schools of nursing in the United States of America, and a member movement of the International Fellowship of Evangelical Students. For information about local and regional activities, write Public Relations Dept., InterVarsity Christian Fellowship/USA, 6400 Schroeder Rd., P.O. Box 7895, Madison, WI 53707-7895, or visit the IVCF website at <www.intervarsity.org>.

Cover design: Cindy Kiple
Interior design: Beth Hagenberg
Images: old notebook cover: © ixer/iStockphoto
fence and fog: © David Stephenson/iStockphoto

ISBN 978-0-8308-3791-5

Printed in the United States of America ∞

Library of Congress Cataloging-in-Publication Data

Gibbs, Eddie.
  The journey of ministry : insights from a life of practice / Eddie Gibbs
    p. cm.
  Includes bibliographical references.
  ISBN 978-0-8308-3791-5 (pbk. : alk. paper)
  1. Church work. I. Title

  BV4400.G53 2012
  253—dc23

                                                                    2012018672

P	18	17	16	15	14	13	12	11	10	9	8	7	6	5	4	3	2	1
Y	27	26	25	24	23	22	21	20	19	18	17	16	15	14	13	12		

*This book is our legacy to our four children,
their spouses and our eight grandchildren:*

Steve and Hiromi

*Rachel and David,
and their daughters, Ashley and Colleen*

*Helen and Joe,
their adult son, Andrew, and younger children,
Emily, Ryan and Maya*

*Linda and Brian,
their daughter, Anika, and son, Tristan*

CONTENTS

FOREWORD

Given the popularity—richly deserved—of his books *LeadershipNext*, *ChurchNext* and *Emerging Churches*, I thought the publisher might call this book *GibbsNext* or *EmergingGibbs*. I, for one, have often wondered what Eddie Gibbs will come up with next, what his emerging project might be. And that wondering has always been accompanied by a desire for more insights from him.

We learn a lot about Eddie in this fine book. But it's not because he simply focuses on himself. Eddie is, for one thing, too much of a family person and colleague for that; his journey of ministry is one shared with many others. But he is also a global Christian, and he has always been very enthusiastic about telling people what God is doing in regions beyond our individual comfort zones. There are many engaging personal reflections in this book, and they point beyond the person who is telling the stories to the much larger narrative of God's creating and redeeming purposes in the world.

Eddie joined the Fuller Theological Seminary faculty in 1984, a year before I arrived to teach. In that sense we are of the same generation in this community. But I've always thought of him as having a younger mind and heart. He is tech savvy, crossculturally experienced, and open to new forms of church life and leadership patterns. At the same time, he is no iconoclast. He has deep spiritual and theological roots. Most of all, his big-picture vision of the kingdom of Christ is grounded in his deep desire to see men and women enter into a personal relationship with Jesus Christ.

For those who have—or ought to have—learned much from Eddie in his previous writings, this book places it all in the context of an intriguing and delightful journey of shared ministry— a ministry that has always anticipated the *next* things that God has in store for us.

Richard Mouw
President, Fuller Theological Seminary

INCLUDING

We Each Have a Place
in the Family

One of the most difficult images relating to the church for many Western Christians is the idea of church as the family of God. This is partly due to the fact that the very idea of family is under pressure in our culture and partly due to our very restrictive idea of family as mom, dad and two kids. I call this the us-four-no-more syndrome.

Now that my wife, Renee, and I are in our seventies with four married children and eight grandchildren, plus all their extended family, we feel more and more like a dynasty. So it's no longer such a big jump to think of the church to which we belong and the churches around the world that we have visited as "the family of God."

Living in South America for five years and visiting those parts of the world where the idea of family is so much closer to what we find throughout the Bible has enriched our understanding immeasurably. The Bible also reminds us of its much broader understanding of family as it speaks of the "household" of God, which includes many more individuals than the immediate family. (More about that in chapter five.)

The New Testament speaks repeatedly of "God the Father of
our Lord Jesus Christ." And Jesus drew his disciples into that
relationship when he taught them to pray, "Our Father in heaven
. . ." (Matthew 6:9). The apostles knew that it was from their
heavenly Father that "all blessings flow." And the apostle Paul
reminds us of how great the privilege of being able to address
God as Father is: "Because you are sons, God sent the Spirit of
his Son into our hearts, the Spirit who calls out, 'Abba, Father.'
So you are no longer a slave, but a son; and since you are a son,
God has made you also an heir" (Galatians 4:6-7). *Abba* is a term
of respectful intimacy, reflecting a familial relationship that
must never be taken for granted or presumed upon.

Perhaps the most expansive understanding of the family of
God is to be found in Paul's letter to the Ephesians: "For this
reason I kneel before the Father, from whom his whole family
in heaven and on earth derives its name" (Ephesians 3:14-15).
In this verse we are reminded simultaneously that all creation
is his "family" because he is Creator of all things. But we are
also reminded that, in the more restricted sense, we are part of
the family brought into being by his unique fatherhood over all
who have come into his family through the reconciling work of
Christ on the cross and the giving of his Spirit.

The picture of God our Father in heaven must not be thought
of in remote terms, as if he were an absentee father. He is always
the father at our side, sensitive to our every need, "the Father of
compassion and the God of all comfort, who comforts us in all
our troubles, so that we can comfort those in any trouble with
the comfort we ourselves have received from God" (2 Corinthians 1:3-4).

For Renee and me, the Bible has been a constant companion.

It has been our guide on life's long journey. On many occasions we could not see beyond the next step. In some places, the going has been rough, yet what we thought was an approaching dead end turned out to be a hidden turning point. We've long since discovered that life doesn't stand still; in fact, the older we get, the more we wish it would slow down just a bit. We have to remind ourselves that our movement keeps our hearts pumping, our joints mobile and our muscles strong.

EVERY FAMILY IS MESSY

The seven chapters that make up this book are not primarily about our family but they have more to do with the family of God, made up of many communities, some of which are very large, with congregations in their thousands, while most are small, with just a handful of people.

From the outset, we want to make clear that every family has a different story. Tragically, many families fall apart; marriage as an institution faces great cultural, economic and relational pressures. Abuse and violence are disturbingly common. Our societies are more diverse and mobile, which results in the loosening and breaking of family ties. Single parenting and blended families lead to loneliness and estrangement for many people, and the church does not have a good track record in relating to singles and those who have resorted to cohabiting.

Against this backdrop, I don't wish to give the impression that the church is an idealistic, problem-free extended family. We are not a model in that sense, but we are a model in being a small, rough-and-ready version. I type the word *model* with a smile as I think back to the balsa wood and paper airplane models I made, which usually crashed on their maiden flight, or of the plastic model kits I assembled, which had glue oozing from their seams and messy paint jobs. The results looked nothing like the perfect examples displayed in the toy shops that had inspired me to save my pocket money.

Just like those plastic models I assembled, our family is a messy model. So is every other family I've come to know. And every church is a messy model, despite the exaggerated claims we may make and the publicity we put out. We could do with more truth in advertising.

A couple of idealistic Christians who had begun to attend a church and were considering becoming members stopped at the pastor's office to make inquiries. In the course of the conversation, the pastor learned that they had a history of moving from church to church. He said to them as they laid out their expectations, "I don't think we are the church for you. You may want to keep on looking, and when you think you have found your ideal church, my advice to you is not to join. In so doing, you might spoil it!"

A DIVERSE FAMILY PORTRAIT

Renee and I have a multiracial family. The two of us and our four children are all Caucasian. But we have a daughter-in-law who is Japanese, born and raised in Tokyo. One of our sons-in-law is mixed race: his mother was Korean and his father is African American. He was adopted into the United States by a childless African-American couple. Another son-in-law is a Mexican American, with members of his family still going back and forth between the United States and Mexico. Six of our grandchildren are consequently of mixed race and are bright and beautiful, and we have one granddaughter who is an adopted African American.

Our family gets together for holiday, birthdays and anniversary celebrations. And we have found that family ties can break through racial stereotypes. In fact, we no longer think of one another as racially different. We recognize that each brings a distinctive contribution to the mix, with his or her culture, personality and gifts. As grandparents, we pray that our family continues to be an example (although an imperfect and vulnerable one) of the reconciling and enriching power of the gospel.

Family is not something that you can preserve intact, for it is not a static institution. Children grow up and move on and out. We have watched our children and some of our grandchildren disperse to further their education and to pursue their careers. And the larger the country, the greater the potential separation.

As a family we have had to face difficult issues from time to time and will no doubt continue to do so. We have each had our missteps. We have experienced times of frustration and anger. One or more has taken a wrong direction for a time, but knew that the door was always open for a long-awaited welcome back.

Along with the many joys, we have experienced heartbreaks: experiencing the aging and deaths of our parents and other relatives; holding our stillborn daughter, Alison, briefly in our arms; receiving news that a son-in-law had been killed in a motorcycle accident on his way to work, just a month before the birth of his first child; and watching our daughter face challenges through twelve years of single parenting before she remarried.

We could have released our pent-up anger against God, shouting, "Why, O God, did you let this happen to us?" And in all honesty, there were times when we cried out in anguish. But, with the Bible as our daily guide, we came across a number of prayers and complaints against God that were even more anguished than our own. These provided timely reminders that God is unshockable and that he invites us to be honest with him at all times and in every circumstance. He knows full well that every time we bury our hurts and harbor resentment, those issues continue to gnaw into our souls and do grievous long-term and even lifelong damage.

We are not an elitist family but a mutually supportive community of strugglers. We hold a wide variety of jobs: student financial service worker, FedEx truck driver, paramedic with a fire department and national security analyst. Our family also includes three homemakers—two of whom work part-time, one as a bookkeeper and the other teaching children with special needs in public schools—because they believe that their call, at least for the time being, is to raise their kids and support them through their years of public schooling. All our children are struggling financially in these difficult economic times. Even though some of their jobs are mundane and routine, they are extraordinary individuals, each with his or her spheres of influence.

We are privileged to have children and grandchildren who are brighter and better educated in public schooling than we were in our day. Yet they love to hear about and benefit from our life experiences and accumulated wisdom, even though most of it may sound like ancient history. Long may they enjoy visiting us, even when we become harder of hearing and less coherent.

A WIDER FAMILY

Yet "family" should never be a closed circle. If we are prepared to take the Bible seriously and learn from cultures that are far more community based, then family is a place of welcome to the neighbor, the stranger, the lonely and the needy. Some of our family members are much better at this than we grandparents. We are nearing that stage in life when we don't get out and about as we once did. But our world has not shrunk as a consequence. It's just quieter some days, and we are on the phone and Internet a good deal more.

So why have I focused on our understanding and experience as a family so much in this introduction? Because it's a microcosm of the larger family of God, with all its diversity and issues. The lessons learned and the heartaches experienced in one sphere translate into others, as I hope to show in the following chapters. Please note that my wife of fifty years would declare that she didn't write a single word of this book. But her contribution is much more profound than being the wordsmith. She has written so much of it by her life.

So without further delay, let's embark on the journey.

1

WALKING

A LIFELONG JOURNEY IN A
DIFFERENT DIRECTION

Whether you turn to the right or to the left, your ears will hear a voice behind you, saying, "This is the way; walk in it."

ISAIAH 30:21

My wife and I had not reached our second birthdays when World War II broke out in Europe. Among our earliest memories are those of sirens wailing, warning of an impending air raid, and of huddling with our families on the steps leading to the basement, waiting for the "all clear" siren to sound. We remember our mothers darning socks and stockings, turning cuffs and collars, and patching holes. Nothing was discarded until it was no longer mendable.

Many years later we were looking through our family photo album with our oldest grandchild, then six, when he noticed that all of the oldest photos were black and white, with many not quite in focus. He suddenly piped up, "Nana, when did the world become colored?" He was nearer the truth than he realized, because those wartime years were gray and dark. Bright colors were few and far between.

During the war, there was strict rationing on most food items and—to the great disappointment of us children—candy, with many peacetime goods no longer available. We had to learn to do without. Then gas was in short supply, and eventually available only for essential services. Not that that impacted our families in any way; although my father was a car mechanic for most of his life, we never had a vehicle. We didn't miss it, though, because we were a walking culture. We could play our games of Kick the Can and cricket in the street safely, with only the occasional warning shout: "Watch out! Car coming!"

In our neighborhood-based culture, everybody knew everybody else on our street. If your games proved to be a nuisance, or if you broke a window, rattled a door or were rude, your parents soon heard about it. When neighbors were sick or infirm, we kids did their shopping and our moms popped in to help in the home or for a friendly chat. That may all sound rather idyllic, but that is how we remember life in our childhood.

Those days are long passed. We now live in the impersonal, highly mobile big cities of today. Until recently Renee and I lived in a townhouse complex in Southern California. But old habits die hard. We still walked the neighborhood, though there was seldom anyone else around apart from those taking their dogs to do their business on someone else's patch of grass. In fact, it's difficult to walk our streets because the sidewalk is narrow and interrupted by driveways. There are no porches on the houses; entrances are at the sides. The first sign of anyone arriving or leaving is the raising or lowering of a garage door.

We were always surprised that our evening walks drew comments, especially about the fact that we walk hand in hand (increasingly for mutual support). One of the residents of our complex stopped us and broke down in tears; she had recently been divorced from an abusive husband.

Although we were members of a housing association consisting of about 140 homes, we could never achieve a quorum of the householders to conduct business at our annual meeting. Such is our culture of individualism and isolation.

But most people around the world today have walking cultures, especially in Africa, Latin America, India, rural China and other areas of Asia. People in those environments relate much more easily to the slow-paced walking culture of the Bible. They walk for a variety of reasons. For many, walking is their only means of getting to and from work. Others are driven by hunger or are refugees fleeing enemies who have burned their homes, or raped the women and taken their children to turn them into child soldiers, or sold them into the sex trade or as slave laborers.

Here in the West, most people walk for pleasure or to burn off calories and keep in shape. These are the "power walkers" or runners, wearing their fashionable athletic apparel, with their smartphones and water bottles. They often walk alone or with others for safety or support, yet remain self-focused, determined and uncommunicative.

We Westerners have a lot to learn from walking cultures. To do this, we have to learn to slow down to walking speed ourselves and to relearn some important lessons in life. This applies not just to ourselves as individuals, but also to the churches of which we are a part.

THE WALKING CULTURE OF THE BIBLE

In this chapter we will roam through many texts, because walking provides the context in which so many of the biblical narratives are set. Individuals, groups, tribes and armies cover thousands of miles of territory on foot. Think of Abram's journey from Babylonia (Iraq) through Haran (Syria) to Palestine. Or Moses' journey with the tribes of Israel from Egypt, through the Sinai Desert and the kingdom states on the eastern side of the Dead Sea, to the Jordan River and across into Palestine to take possession of the land. Think of the conquered people of Jerusalem and Judea being marched by their captors into Babylonia. And these were just the major journeys.

Within this grand narrative, people were constantly on the move, precisely because it was a walking culture. Of course, not every journey was made on foot. No doubt they also traveled by donkey and mule, with the rich and powerful journeying "first class" on horses, in chariots and by camel. (I've seen tourists perched precariously on camels, and it makes me wonder why the people of the Bible didn't choose to walk!)

When we turn to the Gospel accounts of Jesus calling his disciples, we see that their response to his invitation required walking around Galilee and crossing the Sea of Galilee en route to Jerusalem for the annual festivals, as far north as Caesarea Philippi and possibly to Mount Hermon (Syria). Journeys that today take hours, in those days took weeks and even months. But in our haste to get to places more quickly, we may lose out.

The book of Acts is full of journeys, first throughout Judea and Samaria and then as far as Damascus. As the church followed the leading of the Spirit in taking the good news to non-Jews, Paul began his missionary journeys across Turkey and into Europe. As churches became established in the strategic urban centers, Christians fanned out across North Africa and into Asia and Europe. It has been estimated that Paul walked several thousand miles in the course of his many journeys.

In such a culture, metaphors pertaining to walking resonate, carrying rich meaning and significance. When consulting a number of modern translations and paraphrases, I noticed that translators provided a range of words to translate the walking metaphor in more meaningful ways to non-walking Western cultures. The word in the original Greek that means "walking" or "walking about" is translated as "living," "behaving" or "doing," to name a few examples. There are good reasons for this, but some valuable nuances have been lost.

Walking has a further important dimension. The Australian aborigines, an ancient people living so close to and in tune with nature and their ancestors, go on "walkabouts" in the vast, arid Australian bush. This allows them to know the terrain and live in conditions where no Westerner could survive. It seems like a good idea to walk about and become thoroughly acquainted with a location and its strong points as well as its liabilities.

The sons of Korah, to which a group of kingly psalms are attributed, depict Jerusalem as the fortress of God and tell the citizens, "Walk about Zion, go around her, count her towers, consider well her ramparts, view her citadels, that you may tell of them to the next generation" (Psalm 48:12-13). At the time of the writing of this psalm, the city may have been in ruins, with the remains of the towers, ramparts and citadels standing. In that case, the people would have been reminded that things hadn't always been so bad and that God would deliver them again.

Walking cultures have much to teach us. To learn more, I spent time with a concordance just looking up verses with forms of the word *walk*. Here are some of the things I found.

WALKING AS A METAPHOR FOR THE CHRISTIAN LIFE

In the following chapter, we'll be dealing with ten hurdles to progress within the church of Christ. One of these hurdles has to do with people thinking that the gospel is mainly to guarantee them a place in heaven and to ensure a smoother passage through life. However, the New Testament makes it abundantly clear that the gospel is just as concerned with the way we live before death. Conversion is an "about turn" intended to lead to a life that takes a radically different direction.

Repeatedly Jesus warned his disciples that he was about "to be lifted up"—onto the cross or into heaven. Perhaps there is deliberate ambiguity in his statement. "Then Jesus told them, 'You are going to have the light just a little while longer. *Walk* while you have the light, before darkness overtakes you. The man who *walks* in the dark does not know where he is going. Put your trust in the light while you have it, so that you may become sons of light'" (John 12:35-36, emphasis added to forms of *walk* throughout the rest of the book). When walking in darkness, you can't see where you're going or whether hidden enemies are about to pounce.

For the early church, baptism was no rite of passage or social convention. It signified both cleansing from sin and dying to an old way of life that the new believer may begin to walk in new life in Christ. "Don't you know that all of us who were baptized into Christ Jesus were baptized into his death?" Paul wrote. "We were therefore buried with him through baptism into death in order that, just as Christ was raised from the dead through the glory of the Father, we too may live [*walk*] a new life" (Romans 6:3-4). Some Christians dwell on the dying part and don't recognize the wonderful privilege and empowerment of sharing in the Father's glory made ours by Christ. The good news consists in both the saving death of Christ and his saving life.

Living in the midst of a decadent Roman world, the Christians needed to live a way that was markedly different. "Let us behave [*walk*] decently as in the daytime," Paul wrote, "not in

orgies and drunkenness, not in sexual immorality and de-
bauchery, not in dissension and jealousy. Rather, clothe your-
selves with the Lord Jesus Christ, and do not think about how
to gratify the desires of the sinful nature" (Romans 13:13-14).
The two communities should be as different as night and day.
Paul exhorted the churches in Galatia, "So I say, live by the
Spirit, and you will not gratify the desires of the sinful nature"
(Galatians 5:16).

Repeatedly the letters of the New Testament exhort young
churches to demonstrate their newfound faith in their manner
of life. For example, Paul wrote to the church in Ephesus, "For
we are God's workmanship, created in Christ Jesus to do good
works, which God prepared in advance for us to do [literally,
"that we should *walk* in them"]" (Ephesians 2:10).

Our Christian walk is never accompanied by a judgmental
attitude. We walk not in aloof pride but in self-sacrificing love.
Again, in Ephesians, we are exhorted to be "imitators of God,
therefore, as dearly loved children and live a life of love, just as
Christ loved us and gave himself up for us as a fragrant offering
and sacrifice to God" (5:1-2). There is no escaping the force of
these words. Paul was setting an example himself, which challenges modern church leaders who insist that they can separate
their public from their private lives. Most celebrities—
including Christian ones—keep their fans at a distance and
limit their access. But the saints' lives are an open book. "Join
with others in following my example," Paul wrote, "and take
note of those who live [*walk*] according to the pattern we gave
you" (Philippians 3:17).

Paul was constantly in prayer for the believers in Colosse as
elsewhere: "Since the day we heard about you, we have not
stopped praying for you and asking God to fill you with the
knowledge of his will through all spiritual wisdom and under-

standing. And we pray this in order that you may live [*walk*] a life worthy of the Lord and may please him in every way: bearing fruit in every good work, growing in the knowledge of God" (Colossians 1:9-10). We receive Jesus Christ precisely that we might follow Paul's instructions on "how to live in order to please God" (1 Thessalonians 4:1).

Our walk is never done, for there is always more to learn as we walk in company with Jesus. And, writing in old age, John reminds every generation of those who call themselves Christian, "We know that we have come to know him if we obey his commands. The man who says, 'I know him,' but does not do what he commands is a liar, and the truth is not in him. But if anyone obeys his word, God's love is truly made complete in him. This is how we know we are in him: Whoever claims to live in him must *walk* as Jesus did" (1 John 2:3-6). For this reason we need to constantly meditate on the record of Jesus' life and ministry in the four Gospels. Especially in our day, when the Jesus story is either not known or seriously misrepresented, we need to hear again the gospel in the Gospels.

I've presented a barrage of biblical texts in this section to challenge you and me afresh with the need to reestablish the good news in our daily walk, lived both within our immediate family and within our church family.

WALKING PROVIDES LEARNING OPPORTUNITIES

I grew up in the inner city, where walking was mainly restricted to city streets and a nearby park. Seldom did we walk along a country lane, and we never saw a mountain. That was until a new Bible class leader arrived at our church and took on our group of eleven- to fifteen-year-old lads. He was a leading pathologist in the city, with a passion for hiking and rock climbing. He opened a whole new world to his Bible class of inner-city kids, taking groups of us in his car north into the beautiful English Lake District and the rugged mountains of North Wales.

In our youthful enthusiasm, we raced ahead, eager to get to the top, while our experienced walker and climber maintained a slow and steady pace behind. Soon we discovered that we were not as fit and energetic as we had assumed, as he caught up and walked alongside. As we walked, we shared our lives and talked about the issues we were facing in a much less inhibited and self-conscious way than we would have done in more familiar surroundings. I think it had to do with the ever-changing landscape and that we were not looking at each other but at the path ahead.

We city kids were also learning new skills. We consulted the Ordinance Survey map regularly as we learned to read a compass, essential when a thick mist suddenly descended. At times we could see no evidence that we were on a trail, until our leader pointed to two or three stones placed on a larger one as a guide—"cairns," he called them. These signs along the way were completely hidden to our untrained eyes.

Though there is great value in walking together, either literally or metaphorically, as a family or as an intergenerational (and we might add multicultural) group, we need guides. Early in its history, Israel was urged, "Fix these words of mine in your hearts and minds; tie them as symbols on your hands and bind them on your foreheads. Teach them to your children, talking about them when you sit at home and when you *walk* along the road, when you lie down and when you get up" (Deuteronomy 11:18-19).

Sometimes it's appropriate and important to walk alone. We need opportunities for solitary reflection so we can refocus. But it's equally important to walk as a family or as part of a group. Walking links learning with life in a relaxed, intergenerational environment. This is in contrast with formal, classroom learning, in a disconnected environment that is safe for the studious but intimidating to academic underachievers, who might shine in a setting that better suits their learning style.

Walking together provides opportunities to pass learning and wisdom from one generation to another. But the communication is not in one direction, for the older folks can learn from the questions and insights of a younger generation. Walking together means walking alongside others, learning not from remote experts but from people who care for us personally, whom we know and respect.

When we walk, we must always be aware of our surroundings. Our awareness must lead to an appropriate response to the needs we encounter along the way. "He has showed you, O man, what is good. And what does the LORD require of you? To act justly and to love mercy and to *walk* humbly with your God" (Micah 6:8). In contrast to the line from the old chorus, as we walk, the world does not "grow strangely dim in the light of his glory and grace." Rather we see it with greater clarity and are prompted by the love of Christ to do something about the needs we see.

WALKING MAKES US LIFELONG LEARNERS— IF WE KEEP MOVING

Many churchgoers and not a few non-churchgoers regard the baptism of their infants as the requirement to obtain an insurance policy guaranteeing eternal life. The same conviction applies in some denominations that delay baptism until a person makes a profession of faith. After baptism, they believe they have a prebooked reservation in the Banqueting House of Heaven, and so they can continue to live without changing direction or reordering their values and priorities.

The Scriptures provide a very different understanding of

what is entailed in baptism and following Christ. Since the first disciples in Galilee, it means entering a school of lifelong learning in which you didn't choose your classmates. Jesus makes that call. Historically, it's within the intergenerational family where most of life's important lessons are learned. But so many of today's families are shattered, with each person living his or her own schedule. When family structures break down entirely, schoolteachers are expected to fill the family's role. I'm convinced that it's within the church that a multi-generational, multicultural learning environment needs to be cultivated. Such a transition would require a radical overhaul of ministry.

In my family, the learning levels and styles run the gamut. One son-in-law has a PhD from an English university and has been published by a university press here in the United States, two daughters graduated *cum laude* in the California state university system, others have struggled throughout their school career in classroom environments that didn't match their learning style, and some grandkids are just learning to recognize words and put together simple sentences. There is a great deal of interchange across the generations in our extended family, providing a rich learning environment. How challenging it is for kids growing up in divided and dysfunctional families to learn and grow.

I'd like to share a story—one I've often thought would make a good Mr. Bean tale—that brought home to me the reality that I'm a lifelong learner in the journey of life. It involves biking, not walking, but the principles are the same.

I upgraded from a bicycle to a moped during my final year at seminary. By that time Renee and I were newlyweds living some distance from the college. My moped was a French-built, powder-blue Mobylette with a 50cc two-stroke engine.

In the United Kingdom, until you pass your driving test, you
have to display a white plate with a large red *L* on both the front
and the back of your vehicle. When we moved to our parish in
South London, I still had the L plates. They warned other
drivers to give me a wide berth—or encouraged intimidation
by those few individuals who like to taunt. I didn't feel it was
urgent to take my driving test, because my vehicle had no pas-
senger seat, so I was not required to be accompanied by a qualified driver.

This arrangement worked fine until I began to visit the mu-
nicipally owned housing estate, equivalent to "the projects" in
US cities. In approaching the tower blocks, I had to go full
throttle up a steep incline, with my 50cc engine announcing
my arrival to all and sundry. My reception committee consisted
of a group of local loiterers who, seeing me in helmet, goggles
and mandatory clerical collar, shouted, "Here comes Ed the
Rev!" That taunt finally prompted me to take my driving test to
remove the L plates, which would at least bring my prestige up
a notch.

Unfortunately, the day of the appointment for my test was
unusually busy. I conducted a funeral service in the morning
and then looked up the location of the test. It was in an area I
was not familiar with, so I found the road in my London A–Z
map and set off at full speed. On arrival, I was dismayed to
discover that there was no Department of Motor Vehicle office
in sight. I consulted my road listing again. I had missed the fact
that there were two roads of the same name, and the alternative
was some distance away. So I took off at full throttle again.

When I arrived at the office twenty minutes late, the examiner was pacing up and down the sidewalk with clipboard in
hand, understandably annoyed. I apologized, and he instructed
me to ride several times around the block while ensuring that I

made the correct hand signals and took the necessary precautions. He also informed me that at some point he would step out into the road in front of me so that I could demonstrate an emergency stop.

I set off and was soon out of sight around the corner as I took the first left turn and then the next, at which point my two-stroke engine began to sputter and then died. With all the extra mileage, I had run out of gas. Some minutes later I came within sight of my instructor, slowly pushing my Mobylette.

When I explained my predicament, he pointed to a gas station across the road and told me to fill up. Unfortunately it didn't offer two-stroke ready-mix gas, so I had to pour gas then oil into the tank separately and shake the bike to attempt to get them to mix. The result was less than satisfactory. The engine misfired constantly as I proceeded with a succession of kangaroo leaps around the course, which was especially tricky when trying to make the required hand signals at each corner.

My final lurch before coming to a complete standstill at the feet of my examiner was occasioned by the emergency stop I had been forewarned about. I dismounted my machine, removed my helmet and goggles, and undid my jacket, revealing my clerical collar. My instructor licked his pencil and asked me five trick questions, two of which I got wrong. I trailed behind him into his office, dreading the verdict. He took a long time rechecking his list, looked me straight in the eye and after a dramatic pause said, "Passed!" I nearly passed out. And he clearly didn't want to see me again.

With some feeling of guilt, but with great relief, I removed the offending L plates from my Mobylette, but I continue to wear them on my heart. I remain a lifelong learner with no final grades or graduation ceremony until I'm in the presence of my Maker and Savior.

WALKING INCLUDES TELLING OUR STORY

As I type these words, I have in front of me one of my favorite books: *A Walking Guide to the English Lake District*. It's part of a series by Alfred Wainwright, who of all walking-guide authors captures my interest the most. His books are unusual in that they are handwritten in neat pen-and-ink script and copiously illustrated with maps and sketches of views along the walks. They include a step-by-step guide of the route taken for each walk, a 360-degree panorama identifying all the peaks visible at various points (provided you're not surrounded by mist or drenched in rain), and a sketch of the horizon, naming each mountain and hilltop. As a guide, Wainwright is reliable precisely because he has walked those paths and trails himself and invites his readers to pull on their boots and don their gear to share the journey with him.

Psalm 23 is one of my favorite psalms for the same reason. In describing his own journey, David invites us to walk alongside. He begins by reminding us that in his own walk he is not going it alone: "The LORD is my shepherd." Because the words are so familiar to many, let us pause to look at this psalm again from the perspective of walking.

> The LORD is my shepherd, I shall not be in want.
>   He makes me lie down in green pastures,
> he leads me beside quiet waters,
>   he restores my soul.
> He guides me in paths of righteousness
>   for his name's sake.
> Even though I *walk*
>   through the valley of the shadow of death,
> I will fear no evil,
>   for you are with me;

your rod and your staff,
  they comfort me.
You prepare a table before me
  in the presence of my enemies.
You anoint my head with oil;
  my cup overflows.
Surely goodness and love will follow me
  all the days of my life,
and I will dwell in the house of the LORD forever.

David can speak from personal experience of the guiding and protecting presence of his God, who is neither distant nor uncaring. God is the ever-watchful shepherd. Although a shepherd himself, David did not always walk through green pastures and beside quiet waters. He experienced the darkest valleys, in which evil and danger surrounded him. Sometimes darkness envelops us when we have strayed off course, but it may also happen when we are still on the right path. Jesus' own walk led to Gethsemane and the cross.

Some Christians believe that the walk is hard at the beginning but gets easier as you make progress along life's way. But often it becomes more difficult; the path becomes steeper and more hazardous as we progress. A thoughtful reading of Psalm 23 prepares us for such eventualities.

Notice that this psalm is not all about walking; it begins with rest and refreshment. But that image runs contrary to our usual experience. Tired and sleepy walkers can easily lose their balance and their way. The psalm reaches its dramatic climax with a lavish table spread and the anointing oil of blessing, which the psalmist's cup is not big enough to contain. David, who was harassed by enemies for so much of his life, is finally vindicated.

I was speeding along a highway toward my home city, having received a phone call that my father had just had emergency surgery after an aortic aneurysm and was not expected to survive. I arrived at the hospital and was quickly seated by his bed. His eyes were closed and he was unable to speak. I told him who I was and said, "If you can hear me, just squeeze my hand, Dad." I felt the firm grip of his rough mechanic's hand. Then I began to recite Psalm 23: "The Lord is my shepherd . . ." I prayed that he would be able to make them his own. Within a few minutes, he was in the presence of his Maker.

WALKING TESTS OUR OBEDIENCE

Walking at the invitation of another person requires trust, especially when you have no idea of the route you will take or the ultimate destination. In other words, walking is a relational exercise that tests our faith as well as our stamina.

The Bible provides many examples. Think of Abram's (later renamed Abraham) initial, prompt response to God's call. "The LORD had said to Abram, 'Leave your country, your people and your father's household and go to the land I will show you.' . . . So Abram left, as the LORD had told him" (Genesis 12:1, 4). What a heart-wrenching decision that must have been. As the narrative continues, we learn that even Abraham, that great man of faith, strayed off course a number of times and in so doing endangered his family and compromised his witness.

As the people of God prepared to enter the Promised Land— and to face the challenges and temptations of living among peoples with gods and values very different from their own— they were exhorted, "*Walk* in all the way that the LORD your God has commanded you, so that you may live and prosper and prolong your days in the land that you will possess" (Deuteronomy 5:33).

Throughout the history of Israel, the people repeatedly demonstrated a rebellious spirit, but God didn't give up on them. In fact, he repeatedly pleaded with his people to turn back to him. For example, "If my people would but listen to me, if Israel would follow my ways, how quickly would I subdue their enemies and turn my hand against their foes!" (Psalm 81:13-14). He continued not only to exhort them but to teach them. As Isaiah affirmed, "He will teach us his ways, so that we may *walk* in his paths. . . . Come, O house of Jacob, let us *walk* in the light of the LORD" (Isaiah 2:3, 5).

Learning to walk with our God is a lesson of a lifetime. Sick or injured people who have been bedridden for any length of time have to learn to walk again. The same is true for those who have walked away from the Lord or who have become spiritually paralyzed. We all need to heed the voice of correction from time to time. The prophet Isaiah said, "Whether you turn to the right or to the left, your ears will hear a voice behind you, saying, 'This is the way; *walk* in it'" (Isaiah 30:21). God promises to always walk in front of us, and when we are self-willed and going off course, he is never far behind.

WHEN YOU WALK, CHOOSE YOUR PATH CAREFULLY

It's important to learn to discern one voice from another, because there are other voices we hear along the way that will endeavor to entice us to walk in wrong directions, to take wrong turns to follow false gods. The first psalm reminds walkers to be very careful whom they listen to and to avoid at all costs walking "in the counsel of the wicked" (Psalm 1:1). Once we fall in step, we soon find ourselves standing with them and ultimately sitting alongside them, identifying with their mockery of the righteous. This is a gradual but predictable process. It ends in an empty, lifeless and purposeless existence. We become "like chaff that the wind blows away" (verse 4). The psalmist contrasts the way of the wicked with the way of those who delight in the way of the Lord. He reminds us that abundant life does not consist in frenzied activity but in dwelling like a tree planted by streams of water, where it's nourished until it's ready to yield its fruit in season (see verse 3). In this generation that demands instant results, we need to remind ourselves that the timing for fruitfulness is in God's hands and can't be dictated by human striving. The tree prospers in every way because "the LORD watches over the way of the righteous, but the way of the wicked will perish" (verse 6).

I've learned from hill walkers and mountaineers that we need to remain alert and attentive at all times. When walking in the Lake District, I often heard the cry of distressed sheep, especially at nightfall. These are not the timid animals that have remained in the lowland pastures, but the bold ones that have followed their noses to higher ground. Eventually, some of them find themselves trapped on a narrow ledge, unable to move forward or to turn round and return the way they came. If they are not rescued by the shepherd, they eventually die where they stand or fall to the valley below. Boldness does not always translate to wisdom. The same is true of those who mistake folly for faith.

WANDERING AND MARCHING ARE DIFFERENT FROM WALKING

Wandering is aimless walking about—walking with neither a sense of purpose nor evidence of progress. We think of Israel wandering in the Sinai desert for forty years because they were not spiritually prepared for the next stage in their journey. They

conveniently ignored memories of hard labor as they complained to God that they missed the rich and bountiful supplies
of food they had enjoyed in Egypt. They needed a renewed confidence in God's presence going before them to face the coming
conflicts. They needed time to establish their identity in God.
Sometimes wandering is the result of becoming lost or dis-
oriented. At other times it is due to procrastination or a loss of
nerve. During times of prolonged wandering, sheer survival becomes the key consideration. As the psalmist wrote, "For you,
O LORD, have delivered my soul from death, my eyes from tears,
my feet from stumbling, that I may *walk* before the LORD in the
land of the living" (Psalm 116:8-9).

And a time of wandering may be necessary to prepare us for
the next stage of the journey. Writing in a context of religious
confusion, the prophet Hosea asked, "Who is wise? He will realize these things. Who is discerning? He will understand
them. The ways of the LORD are right; the righteous *walk* in
them, but the rebellious stumble in them" (Hosea 14:9).

Marching is entirely different from wandering. It requires
obedience and strict discipline. Armies march; they don't
wander about. When they are well trained, disciplined and fit,
they keep perfectly in step and in ranks. They respond as one
body to every command. At least, that is how it's supposed to be.

I was in the military for just two years, and I was not a good
marcher. You see, I'm not very coordinated. I dreaded the slow
march because I had difficulty keeping my balance, and my
greatest trauma was in trying to return my bayonet to its
scabbard using the required series of positions.

On one occasion I missed completely, and the weapon
crashed to the ground. Fortunately, the drill sergeant didn't
hear the noise over the din of his own bellowing of commands.
But then, to my horror, he immediately ordered a right turn and

marched us to the edge of the parade ground before doing an
about turn. There was my bayonet in full view. But the good
Lord must have afflicted him with temporary blindness; apparently he didn't see it lying there. We returned to the exact spot,
and while his back was turned, I retrieved the bayonet and put
it safely to its scabbard.

THE PROBLEM OF
MILITARY-MINDED PASTORS

Some controlling pastors regard their congregations in military terms, as-
suming they must be ordered and organized. They want them to march in
step, so they develop a variety of programs through which people are intended to progress from stage to stage in their Christian life. The problem
is that each person is at a different stage, facing different situations and
moving at a different pace. Helping a congregation *walk* together instead
is a much better strategy.

Then there was the occasion of the annual Battle of Britain
parade, when our entire camp marched through the town re-
splendent in our most formal dress Royal Air Force (RAF) uniforms. But we soon encountered a problem. At the front of the
column was a contingent of the Women's Royal Air Force that
took shorter steps than the men behind. Every few minutes we
received the order to "change step" to appear to be marching in
unison. The situation deteriorated as the clatter of boots on
cobbled, narrow streets reverberated from the sides of buildings.

When we went on walks as a family, we did not—and could
not—expect military precision, yet we also could not just
wander around. Our asthmatic child sometimes struggled, or
one or more of the children complained of not liking to walk,

or someone wore the wrong shoes and got blisters, or the youngest lagged behind or insisted on scampering ahead. My wife and I came to a fresh appreciation of Moses' leading of thousands through and around the Sinai wilderness for forty years. No wonder they were organized in tribes and extended families to ensure some form of control and provide a degree of protection.

Trouble and danger have surrounded God's people in many stages of their journeys through life, not only in the wilderness of Sinai but also as they walked across the desert to Babylonia. And we, like them, are in God's hands as we walk together: "Though I *walk* in the midst of trouble, you preserve my life; you stretch out your hand against the anger of my foes, with your right hand you save me" (Psalm 138:7).

WE WALK EITHER BY FAITH OR IN FOLLY

Abram had no idea of his ultimate destination when he set out in obedience to the Lord's command. It was the same for the first followers of Jesus when he called them to leave their nets, their families and their livelihood as fishermen. Up to that time, their lives had been associated with the Sea of Galilee. Then along came Jesus and invited them (I suspect with a look that does not take no for an answer), saying, "Come, follow me, . . . and I will make you fishers of men." They obeyed without question or procrastination. "At once they left their nets and followed him" (Mark 1:17-18).

The alternative pathway—going our own way—is the more popular of the two directions in which to walk. The lemmings always outnumber the pilgrims. The Bible provides disturbing evidence that this holds true even among those who number themselves among his people. Isaiah speaks for God, who says, "All day long I have held out my hands to an obstinate people, who *walk* in ways not good, pursuing their own imaginations" (Isaiah 65:2). They are determined to go their own way, infatuated by their fantasies, misguided thoughts and crooked schemes.

Isaiah encourages us not to live independently of God: "Let him who *walks* in the dark, who has no light, trust in the name of the LORD and rely on his God. But now, all you who light fires and provide yourselves with flaming torches, go, *walk* in the light of your fires and of the torches you have set ablaze" (Isaiah 50:10-11). If we walk by our own light, we get more than our fingers burned.

DELAYED JOURNEYS AND LEARNING TO WAIT

Abram was ninety-nine years old when the Lord appeared to him and said, "I am God Almighty; *walk* before me and be blameless. I will confirm my covenant between me and you and will greatly increase your numbers" (Genesis 17:1-2). Abram was well into his journey when he received this word from the Lord. It had begun in his own country of Babylon (Iraq) as he left the security of his extended family and familiar surroundings to go to a land that the Lord had promised to show him, but which had not yet been revealed.

There are other instances of God calling individuals later in life. Sometimes the delay resulted from their frustration and impetuosity. For example, Moses intervened on behalf of a fellow Israelite by killing an Egyptian slave master. But his own people resented his initiative and he feared the wrath of Pharaoh, so he fled.

Isaiah reminds both his own generation as well as today's youth that "even youths grow tired and weary, and young men stumble and fall; but those who hope in the LORD will renew their strength. They will soar on wings like eagles; they will run and not grow weary, they will walk and not be faint" (Isaiah 40:30-31). Yet we can't expect to soar all of the time. We have to learn to slow down, from soaring to running to walking and then to rest.

INVITING OTHERS TO WALK WITH US

Our walk is never for the sake of self-fulfillment, but so that countless other people might be blessed as we walk among them. Abram was guaranteed this at the outset, despite the fact that the promise was tantalizingly vague: "I will make you into a great nation and I will bless you; I will make your name great, and you will be a blessing. I will bless those who bless you, and whoever curses you I will curse; and all peoples on earth will be blessed through you" (Genesis 12:2-3). Even today, thousands of years later, that promise is only partially fulfilled, despite the fact that Israel—and then the church—received constant reminders of its spiritual and moral responsibilities to the wider world.

In the commissioning of the disciples, who had been apostles in training, Jesus translated those reminders into a command, which we know as the Great Commission:

All authority in heaven and on earth has been given to me. Therefore go and make disciples of all nations, baptizing them in the name of the Father and of the Son and of the Holy Spirit, and teaching them to obey everything I have commanded you. And surely I am with you always, to the very end of the age. (Matthew 28:18-20)

Will we walk into that call?

QUESTIONS FOR THOUGHT AND DISCUSSION

1. What lessons have you learned from your experience of

family over the years? Have you taken the opportunity to pass on the lessons learned from painful or stressful times as well as from joyful celebrations? Have you had to deal with heart-rending tragedies? Where did you find support at such times?

2. As a follower of Jesus wearing an L plate of a lifelong learner, what lessons have you had to learn in recent years, and who or what helped you to learn those lessons?

3. Have there been times when you have wandered from the path, either deliberately or accidentally? Consider those times when you could only see one step ahead, if that, and contrast them with times when you could see far into the distance.

4. Describe an experience when you have either felt frustration because church leaders have attempted to regiment and control you, or when you have been encouraged and enriched as you have journeyed with fellow pilgrims in the life of faith.

5. Who have you shared your journey with and been grateful to have at your side during times when you needed support? Who have you supported?

2

HURDLING

NAMING AND OVERCOMING
OBSTACLES TO PROGRESS

By my God I can leap over a wall.

PSALM 18:29 NRSV

Among all the track and field events, hurdling and steeple-chasing present the most obstacles to the athlete. Running an obstacle course requires focus, precision and stamina. Although it is not as daunting as pole vaulting, which requires unhesi-tating commitment and all-out effort, hurdling requires focus not just on the hurdle immediately confronting you, but on a succession of equally challenging obstacles. (In some ways, the steeplechase presents an even more accurate analogy to the spiritual life, in that every obstacle is different and presents a unique challenge.)

Life is like running hurdles, with the way ahead cluttered with challenging obstacles. It's hazardous to run blindfolded through life; its hurdles can neither be ignored nor denied. We also can't assume that we have the strength to knock the hurdles

down rather than jump over them, for sooner or later we will
stumble and fall.

In hurdling, failures are not final. If you hit a hurdle, you can
keep running. If you fall, you can get back up again. Our oldest
grandson, Andrew, is a hurdler, so he has supplied me with
some knowledge of the sport and some hurdling stories to tell.
Andrew's coach taught him the keys to success in hurdling:
You need to develop stamina, stamina and more stamina. It's
no use giving an all-out effort only to fade at the end. Make
sure your starting block position feels comfortable to you, and
use that position every time. Never "stutter step," or take
short, choppy steps, because you will lose ground and momentum. Never settle for your fastest time. Always dip your
head in at the finish. If you find yourself out of position, go
with the "wrong" leg, even if it feels uncomfortable. Never
focus on any other racer than yourself, and don't be intimidated by another racer.

We can review the coach's advice and see both the strength
and limitations in the hurdling image when we apply it to life.
For example, Special Olympians have also taught us to be
mindful of other runners, stepping out of the race to help them
up, even if it means that we lose. If we should stumble or fall,
we need the courage to get up and resume the race. We also
need to recognize that throughout life we learn more from our
failures than from our successes.

Our grandson shared the following hurdling experience
with us:

> At the start of one race we had a good jump out of the
> blocks, but the umpire called a false start, so we had to
> start the race over again. Then with the restart of the race,
> I was a bit tired so my footing was off and I tripped over

the first hurdle. On impact with the ground, I thought I had dislocated my shoulder, and I lay on the ground for what seemed a good amount of time. But I heard the coach in my mind saying, "Don't quit!" On hearing that, I got up and ran my heart out. Not only did I finish the race, but I came in third out of the eight!

After I had run out of all my energy, the coach came up to me and asked me if I wanted to run the 4x4 relay. I said, "Sure," not knowing what I was getting myself into. Listening to what the coach had said about not focusing on myself, I didn't care whether this was my event or whether it was theirs. And out of the block I just went and ran the fastest 400-meter I have ever run, and ultimately my team took the win.

THREE CATEGORIES OF HURDLES CHURCHES FACE TODAY

Churches face three categories of hurdles today in Western society: individualism, consumerism and nominalism. Under each category, we can identify a number of different hurdles that need to be named and addressed. We can't take these in isolation, just as the hurdler has to take in the entire course ahead in order to establish a rhythm and pace.

Every illustration has its limitations, and the problem with using a sports analogy is that most nonathletes regard themselves as supporters and fans rather than participants. But when the apostle Paul wrote to the growing network of churches in Asia Minor (modern southwest Turkey), he didn't confine his letter to a select group of spiritual athletes, but to all "the saints." In his mind, the saints were not the spiritual elite—an ecclesiastical version of the Olympic athlete. They were the regular folks who made up each local congregation. Their home-based churches were small, consisting of twenty to forty persons at most, so everyone was expected to participate.

HURDLES ASSOCIATED WITH INDIVIDUALISM

Paul's response: Establish and maintain unity (see Ephesians 4:1-6).

The entrepreneurial, pioneering spirit of North America has produced one of the most individualistic cultures in the world. In modern times, especially after World War II, we moved on to hyper-individualism as families were scattered during the suburban housing boom, as educational and business opportunities presented themselves and as the focus on self-realization became a pervasive cultural assumption.

Hurdle 1: Self-preoccupation. Some families and churches believe that commitment to Christ and to the resources and protection of his grace ensures immunity from life's troubles, traumas and tragedies. Their response to adversity can be angry: "Why has God allowed this to happen to us?" Immediately they interpret events and their immediate and anticipated consequences in personal terms.

Such a self-centered attitude needs to be contrasted with that of the apostle Paul. He wrote several of his letters, not from the comfort of a hospitable home or a hotel, but from prison. This situation is bad for anyone, but especially for someone whose calling is that of an apostle. Apostles are driven by the conviction and passion that they have been called by the risen Christ himself to be continually on the move, breaking new ground. In his journeys around the northern Mediterranean, Paul was shuttling back and forth to encourage the recently formed communities of new and vulnerable believers. Many of these groups had come into being through his own evangelistic initiatives, while others were the result of local leaders following his example.

Now he lay in prison, either in Ephesus or Rome. His ministry, if not in limbo, was severely restricted. We don't know to what extent he was allowed visitors. However, his imprisonment provided him with an opportunity to write letters. We have four examples preserved in the New Testament, known as the prison epistles: Ephesians, Philippians, Colossians and the highly significant personal letter to Philemon. It concerns the return of Philemon's runaway slave, Onesimus, who somehow found Paul in Ephesus and became a true believer. Paul wrote that Onesimus "became my son while I was in chains. Formerly he was useless to you, but now he has become useful both to you and to me" (Philemon 10-11).

Though Paul reminded his readers throughout these letters that he had been incarcerated, his focus was not on himself, but rather on the growing network of Christian extended households. He was constantly concerned for the spiritual progress of the believers in Ephesus, as well as other locations where this letter circulated. He was burdened that they should remain "faithful in Christ Jesus" (Ephesians 1:1). He described them as "chosen" or called by Christ. He writes, as a prisoner of the Lord, "I urge you to live a life worthy of the calling you have received" (4:1).

Why was his exhortation so urgent? It arose on account of the state of humanity—not just in the first century but also today. In the lead-up to the fourth chapter, Paul emphasized the need for an alienated humanity to be reconciled to God and to one another, and he presented the glorious vision of a new humanity brought into being as people respond wholeheartedly and in every area of life to the presence of Jesus among them by his Spirit that indwells each believer and faith community. Such was the intensity and breadth of his vision that it overrode his personal circumstances. He longed for his readers, then as now, to experience a similar liberation from self-preoccupation and self-pity.

Hurdle 2: Elitism. One of the problems with elitism is that people who think they are a cut above the rest are prone to take themselves too seriously. But God has his own way of humbling us from time to time. For instance, I claim the unrecorded world record for the Worst Missionary Meeting Ever.

It all began when the general secretary of the mission for whom I worked called me to say that he was due to speak at a meeting that evening but had come down with a heavy cold and had lost his voice. Would I stand in for him? This was a daunting task for a number of reasons. He was a nationally known, entertaining speaker, and I was the last-minute substitute.

I went to his home, where he instructed me that he had planned to speak on his visit to five South American countries, illustrating his talk with a big box of photographic slides. I had visited those countries, but had not been with him on his most recent trip. I thought I could keep a storyline going with the help of the slides. Unfortunately, there was no time to preview them; I had to leave immediately because I would have to battle traffic on the old North Circular Road around London.

I had not been to the church before and was unfamiliar with the location. Traffic was slow, and I missed a turn into the commuter village where the church was. At last I arrived in the church parking lot twenty minutes late to the sound of hearty hymn singing as the people in the packed hall awaited the arrival of the well-known speaker. I ran across the parking lot and arrived breathlessly at the church hall, where I tripped and dropped the box of slides. They scattered across the floor.

I got through the talk as best I could, not knowing what the next slide would be—or even what country it was taken in. Yes, there are some situations that are beyond saving. It was both embarrassing to the nth degree and hilarious; fortunately, it was a happy, spirited crowd. It was an evening the congregation would long remember and one I will too—which is just as well, because a few months later Renee and I were living in that area and attending that church.

Again, Paul's reference to the "called" is not restricted to a few especially chosen, perfect and appointed individuals in each church. They are not the saints who have earned halos, but rank-and-file believers who take their faith seriously. It's not until the middle section (Ephesians 4:7-12) that Paul identified specific callings. Here it's the call of the gospel to live in a way that is in contrast to so much accepted behavior in a degenerate society. He listed the vital signs that should be evident in the lives of those who profess to follow Christ. They make a helpful checklist to bring regularly before God in prayer.

• *Humility:* an appreciation of the worth and contribution of others. Contrast the superior attitude described by Paul in writing to some proud and independent Corinthians, who declared, "I don't need you!" (1 Corinthians 12:21).

• *Gentleness:* not a sign of weakness and compliance but of inner strength. It does not suggest an attitude of inferiority to those we look up to and desire to emulate that says, "I don't have those gifts, so I don't belong to the body." (See 1 Corinthians 12:14-30, where Paul expanded on this point.)

• *Patience:* putting up with annoying people and frustrating circumstances, trying to understand why they rub us the wrong way. We don't choose our Christian companions, just as we don't choose our family members. So we had better learn to get along together.

• *Bearing with one another,* which the New Living Translation renders as "making allowance for each other's faults" (Ephe-

sians 4:2). If the gospel is a message that brings reconciliation, we need to demonstrate its reconciling power among
the members of the body of Christ.

- *Love:* putting all of the above into practice. Paul is not re-
ferring to warm feelings of affection but to self-giving,
initiative-taking love, demonstrated by God himself in his
love for the world and by Jesus in laying down his life on our
behalf.

I remember well the Argentine pastor Juan Carlos Ortiz
challenging a group of missionaries at a retreat, saying that we
pick and choose our favorite texts of Scripture. He asked how
many of us had underlined the most well-known verse in the
Bible: "For God so loved the world that he gave his one and only
Son, that whoever believes in him shall not perish but have
eternal life" (John 3:16). He then asked us to look up 1 John
3:16 to see how many of us had underlined that verse. It's an
almost identical reference, but with a different message: "This
is how we know what love is: Jesus Christ laid down his life for
us. And we ought to lay down our lives for our brothers." No
hands were raised this time, and the room was silent.

Hurdle 3: Complacency. Individualism leads to constant
jockeying for position as well as reluctance to be moved out of
a comfort zone. Most complacent people are content with the
status quo, or they aren't content but have simply moved to the
sidelines. Theirs is a shoulder-shrugging, why-bother attitude.

Paul had no tolerance for complacency. He recognized that
unity can't be taken for granted. Issues must not be swept under
the carpet and divisions papered over through either denial or
avoidance. He required his fellow Christians to "make every
effort to keep the unity of the Spirit through the bond of peace"
(Ephesians 4:3). A complacent church is in no state to proclaim

so radical and urgent a message as the good news of Jesus Christ. And a divided church has lost all credibility to proclaim a message of reconciliation.

Are we being presented with a depressingly impossible ideal? From the outset we must admit that these qualities can't be manufactured but only realized through the presence of God in our midst. They are the outcomes of the initiatives of our heavenly Father, who created the family in the first place. They are the fruit of the Lord Jesus Christ, who carried out his Father's mission at unfathomable personal cost and continues his ministry of intercession on our behalf. They are the fruit of the Holy Spirit, who indwells us personally and corporately. The three Persons of the Trinity don't act independently but with interdependence. They are one God in three Persons, forming a community of being over all and through all and in all. We hear and heed Paul's exhortations "I urge you" and "make every effort," and we dare not hold back, duck or walk away.

The New Testament concept of the church challenges Western individualism in its stress on the church as family and on the fact that we are made sons and daughters in that family by the process of adoption. Furthermore, the Holy Spirit bears witness within us of our new status as God's adoptees. And by him we cry, "Abba, Father" (Romans 8:15; see also v. 23; Ephesians 1:5). We are not simply adopted into a one-on-one relationship with our heavenly Father, but into the family inaugurated by Christ.

The relational aspect of the church is further reinforced by Paul's, James's, Peter's and John's frequent reference to fellow believers as brothers and sisters in Christ (for example, see Romans 1:13; James 2:15, 1 Peter 1:22; 1 John 3:16). The term these New Testament writers actually used is *brother*, but the word refers both to male and to female. It also has a wider connotation than just siblings, including others within the extended family, such as cousins and other kin. This underlines the intimacy of the relationship that Christians have with one another. A feeling of embarrassment when kinship terms are used is evidence of the prevailing individualism and a reluctance to enter into a deep relationship with other believers.

In the church, as in a family, we are often mindful of the particular hurdle that each person is facing or that the community is facing together. But unlike hurdles on a track, hurdles in life are not identical and neither are they spaced evenly. We are here to assist one another when a particular hurdle seems insurmountable. The objective is not to win the race, but to complete the course with each other's support and encouragement.

HURDLES ASSOCIATED WITH CONSUMERISM

Paul's response: Encourage the participation of every member, according to his or her gifts, calling and passion (see Ephesians 4:7-12).

Consumerism not only drives Western economies, it also permeates and subverts the faith of Christians and the assumptions on which many churches base their approach to ministry. The false identification of affluent living with quality of life is one of the biggest heresies of our time, and it's not only assumed but also promoted in many congregations, both large and small.

Such a materialistic attitude stands in contrast to that of the early church, as well as to rapidly growing churches in non-Western societies where there is little to consume. Just surviving from day to day is their overriding concern. Yet possessions are given freely; in places such as rural Africa, Christmas is not a time for lavish gift giving, but for drawing on meager food supplies to create a community feast.

In Ephesians 4:7-12, Paul addressed the issue head-on, and we have to read this first-century text through twenty-first-century eyes. Here, in contemporary terms, are some of the issues consumerism causes. **Hurdle 4: Opting out.** Many in the pews are content to leave all aspects of ministry to the experts. After all, are they not the ones trained and paid for by the congregation to satisfy their needs and meet their expectations? If their leaders fail to deliver "the goods," consuming churchgoers are ready to move elsewhere. But church membership, as understood in New Testament terms, was not joining a club and paying your dues in order to enjoy the benefits of membership. The word *member* refers to a limb or organ in the body with its own location and vital function in that location.

Paul's response to passive recipients or grumblers was clear and unequivocal: "But to *each* one of us grace has been given as Christ apportioned it" (Ephesians 4:7). This is just one of several occasions when he returned to the theme of ministry being carried out by every member playing his or her part. In every instance, the word *each* appears.

Paul cautioned the Christian church in Rome not to adopt a superior attitude that would disempower others. Every person, whatever his or her rank, age or intellectual capacity, has a vital role to play in the body of Christ. "Just as *each* of us has one body with many members, and these members do not all have the same function, so in Christ we who are many form one body, and each member belongs to all the others" (Romans 12:4-5).

The same message is conveyed to the Christians in Corinth, to whom Paul wrote, "Now to *each* one the manifestation of the Spirit is given for the common good." He then went on to identify a selection of gifts, with the summary, "All these are the work of one and the same Spirit, and he gives them to each

one, just as he determines" (1 Corinthians 12:7, 11).
Paul was not alone in his exhortation. Peter, in his letter addressed to churches in Asia Minor, urged everyone to get involved: "*Each* one should use whatever gift he has received to serve others, faithfully administering God's grace in its various forms" (1 Peter 4:10). When individuals opt out, they not only impoverish themselves but they deprive the church of essential service, and its witness in the world is seriously restricted and undermined. We either use it or lose it. What is holding us back from using our gifts, and who are we depriving?

To put it more bluntly, if we persist in refusing to exercise the abilities and calling that arise from the grace of Christ in our lives, we are not *members* of the body but *parasites* feeding on it and weakening it. That statement is not intended to send anyone on a guilt trip, because all too frequently it's not the fault of the individual. He or she may not have opted out, but may have been overlooked or excluded because of restrictive practices exercised by leaders who feel threatened by initiatives and resources other than their own.

For two successive years, I had the privilege of meeting with younger church leaders in Philadelphia by leading a seminar with an African American pastor in the city. He was also a sociologist who commuted to Washington, D.C., to teach at Howard University, which has a predominantly black student body. We each addressed the challenge of consumerism from our different perspectives. I learned from him that it was just as much a problem in African American denominations. To illustrate his point, he told the following story: There were two families shopping in the same supermarket who came face-to-face in the same aisle. One mother smiled at the other and said, "I'm sure we have met somewhere before. Would you mind turning around for a moment? I think we go to the same church."

Hurdle 5: Loss of nerve. Controversy swirls around the term *apostle.* This has arisen partly because it is used for two distinct groups in the New Testament. In Luke's Gospel and in his book of Acts, it's used almost exclusively to describe the Twelve (with just one exception in Acts 14:14). This is the first group of disciples, who were selected by Jesus for training in apostolic ministry and knew him personally. All but Judas encountered the risen Christ before his ascension. They formed the foundation pillars of the new people of God, corresponding to the twelve tribes of Israel.

Paul used the term in a different sense. For him, they were never "the twelve," but rather they were pioneer missionary church planters. He mentioned ten by name, including one who is possibly female, Junia, although some translations opt for the masculine form, Junias (see Romans 16:7).

With the collapse of Christendom in many parts of the Western world, the church in the twenty-first century needs to rediscover the importance of apostolic groundbreakers. Without their contribution, the church is unlikely to penetrate the surrounding pluralistic and increasingly neopagan culture

The apostle goes where the church has yet to penetrate or to areas it has abandoned or in which it finds itself ignored or excluded. Modern-day apostles are groundbreaking in the worlds of politics, business, education and entertainment.

The apostle must not be confused with the resourceful entrepreneur, operating out of human ego. Apostles are literally "sent ones" who are responding to the call of God. They are driven by an unquenchable passion in their restless quest to break new ground. Apostles might be rough around the edges and not always polite, and they are typically difficult to work with due to their independent spirit and restless energy.

Hurdle 6: Becoming bland. Much of the Western church

today is preoccupied with being politically correct—saying what it thinks the culture wants to hear. When it adopts this stance, it finds itself continually trying to catch up with yesterday, with little sense of where the pathway may be leading. Its voice becomes more like an echo reverberating from the surrounding hills or tall buildings. Little wonder the church's voice, when it has one at all, can be conveniently ignored. We are finally reduced to talking to ourselves, because few others take an interest in what we have to say.

Political correctness is not a new phenomenon. We have only to read through the history of Israel from the time of the appearance of her first prophets. We discover that those who listened to God and spoke out in his name constantly had to battle the "politically correct" false prophets who affirmed the direction leaders were taking on every point. These false prophets exercised influence on the elite and attempted to silence the challenges of the authentic prophet, either by marginalizing them or silencing them completely. In the same way, a bland church simply baptizes the culture, affirming its direction.

The role of the authentic prophet, both before the coming of Christ and within the early church, was central to the proclamation of the truth. John the Baptist was the last in the long line of Old Testament-type prophets, and nobody could accuse him of being bland! But notice that he didn't prophesy in Jerusalem, the center of Jewish hopes and religious influence. He conducted his ministry by the River Jordan, on the very borders of Israel and non-Jewish lands, and crowds came from all parts of the country to his desert location.

What was so significant about John's chosen spot? It was the very place where centuries before the tribes of Israel had entered the Promised Land. He was signaling to his generation the need for their nation to turn back to God in genuine repentance. His ministry of baptism in the Jordan was a cleansing and a fresh start—a repossession of the land. The times were urgent, not just because of political and social realities, but because the Messiah was about to begin his public ministry among them.

Jesus himself initiated his ministry by identifying with John (who incidentally was his cousin), and much to John's embarrassment insisted on being baptized along with the others. This was Jesus' profound act of identity with his generation—and the first step that ultimately led to Jerusalem and his crucifixion.

John the Baptist's message emphasized the coming of the kingdom of God, but not in nationalistic terms. On the contrary, it came as a threat to his nation's religious self-preoccupation and its political accommodation to Roman overlords. He later took the perilous and bold step of charging King Herod Antipas with an illegal marriage and with attempting to extend his power of influence through his brother's wife. John's outspoken protest eventually led to his imprisonment and beheading.

The real Jesus is far from the meek and mild image that many of us have grown up with. Like John the Baptist, he proclaimed the coming of the kingdom, already inaugurated in his person. But with Jesus the kingdom was *good news* rather than a threat. His primary audience was the marginalized in society—the overwhelming majority, crushed by the legalism and ritualism of the religious elite.

Jesus' message and his entire ministry were profoundly subversive. He was walking in a minefield most of the time. From the outset, his days of public ministry were numbered, and they lasted just three short years. But he knew that the timing was not in the hands of his powerful enemies, but in the almighty hands of his heavenly Father, who determined the appointed hour.

By individualizing Jesus' message (which must not be confused with the need to personalize his message) and by turning the gospel into a personal insurance policy for life beyond the grave, we have made the good news bland. No wonder our enfeebled message has so little to say to our generation. When the church's voice in the marketplace is silenced or lost in the babble, it can be ignored. We are left to talk to ourselves.

Alternatively, when frustration mounts and anger can no longer be contained within our ranks, we appear as ugly protesters and placard-waving slogan shouters. The battle lines are drawn between the opposing sides, with the police trying to keep the two sides from each other's throats. The opposite of bland is not confrontation but engagement. Protest might be more an indication of our insecurity than of our faith in the transforming power of the good news. The early church witnessed in its day with boldness and grace. These two vital qualities are much in evidence in our own day in areas of the world where Christian communities face persecution.

We need to recognize that the role of the prophet has changed significantly from the days of the Old Testament prophets. They could address the nation with the bold proclamation "Thus says the Lord" because Israel was not a secular state, but one that ostensibly acknowledged its allegiance to the God who had called it into existence in the first place.

When we move to the New Testament, the role of the prophet changes again. As the church spread rapidly beyond the borders of Israel, congregations were increasingly non-Jewish and lived within a Roman world that was tolerant of other religions, provided they didn't challenge the authority of Caesar, who was the one true lord. For the church to proclaim "Jesus is Lord" (Romans 10:9; 1 Corinthians 12:3) was political dynamite in the Roman world, just as its message of an alternative vision of the kingdom of God was perilous within Israel.

The rapidly growing network of Jesus' followers around the Mediterranean world and beyond needed access to reliable information regarding Jesus, to whom they had committed their personal and corporate lives. Especially in those predominantly Gentile areas, the Hebrew Scripture may not have been readily available. Furthermore, many of the New Testament letters and Gospels had not yet been written, and those that had were in short supply; hand copying is a laborious procedure. The churches were therefore dependent on oral sources.

The four Gospels are a unique form of literature. They outline the teachings and ministry of Jesus but pay particular attention to his final weeks leading to his crucifixion and the empty tomb announcing to the world his rising from the dead. Then they climax with his ascension into heaven, when he handed over his mission to his disciples.

The letters addressed to the New Testament churches clarify key issues of Christian belief, warning against false apostles and prophets who were leading churches astray and dealing with pressing pastoral issues in which guidance, correction and encouragement were needed.

Prophecy needs to be rooted in biblical revelation, relating to God's wider salvation purposes, thereby avoiding degenerating into declarations that are trivial and bland. Prophecy has had a long, checkered history in the life of the church. Sometimes the words of the so-called prophets become power plays and spiritual blackmail. The word of the prophet requires church leaders to exercise spiritual discernment in their response.

Today the role of the prophet has changed again. A prophetic word is not a new revelation, but a fresh understanding or contemporary application. Prophets also remind the churches today of biblical truths that are being neglected or denied. They bring a renewed sense of urgency. When the prophetic voice falls silent, the impression is given that God spoke only in past times to people in distant lands. But there is no long-term future for this bland brand of Christianity in today's Western society, which is increasingly pluralistic, questioning and hostile.

Hurdle 7: Keeping the good news to ourselves. Many churches, especially those that trace their history back to the state churches of Europe, have marginalized the role of the evangelist. Evangelists are gifted individuals who publicly proclaim the good news. A few are most effective in addressing large crowds, whereas the vast majority make greater long-term impact in conversation with smaller groups or one-on-one.

When we attempt to define what an evangelist is, we tend to place almost exclusive emphasis on the pronouncement of the core content of the gospel—the death, resurrection and ascension of Christ—and the need for a response of repentance and faith. These foundational truths of the good news as proclaimed by the early church are the major themes that need to be heralded (the literal meaning of *evangel*) or broadcast.

We also place emphasis on the noun *evangelist*, though the person of the evangelist is mentioned only two other times in the New Testament while the verb "to evangelize" occurs with great frequency.

Finally, we give much less attention to what is sometimes unfortunately mistranslated as *secret*, but which occurs twenty-eight times in the New Testament: God's initiative in Christ, revealing the good news. This might occur through the methodical teaching and explanation of the preacher, but it can also be an "aha!" experience prompted by the Holy Spirit, mediated either directly by God or through a medium of communication.

So much of our evangelistic heritage in North America, and

to a lesser extent in Europe, has been deeply and pervasively influenced by revivalism. Because the church in the West was dominant over a thousand years of Christendom, it was widely assumed that people knew the Bible stories, the main events of the life of Christ and his claims to be the Son of God. The task of the revivalist, whether itinerant or ministering regularly within a local congregation, was to stir the memories of the lapsed and the consciences of the backsliders, challenging them to respond with a clear first-time decision or a recommitment to Christ.

But times have changed to a dramatic extent within the past four decades. The vast majority of people don't know the Grand Narrative of Scripture and have little knowledge of Jesus. In many situations, the only safe assumption the evangelist can make is that the listener knows nothing or that what he or she does know is seriously amiss.

The Bible recognizes the diversity of gifts distributed through local congregations. Most of us are not gifted as evangelists, but we should be part of evangelizing communities, ready and able when the opportunity arises to speak of the transforming power of the gospel in our lives. "But in your hearts set apart Christ as Lord. Always be prepared to give an answer to everyone who asks you to give the reason for the hope that you have" (1 Peter 3:15). If we have nothing to communicate to our surrounding community and the wider world, we might as well go out of business.

The bold, gracious and vibrant witness of churches made up of new immigrants increasingly challenges Western Christians. They represent the changing face of Christianity, not only in North America but also in many parts of Europe. They are the most significant mission movement in the twenty-first century, and they don't have white faces and financial backing.

Like most people of my generation who were trained for local church ministry in the Church of England, I was prepared theologically and pastorally to function with a reasonable degree of competence in all aspects of parish ministry. This extended not just to the congregation that gathered Sunday by Sunday, but also to the wider community that made up a busy London parish, most of which looked to the church for support during sickness and financial crises and for the church to supply rites of passage when they wanted a "white wedding" in church, a baby christened or a loved one buried. I called these "the hatched, matched and dispatched" contingent. One of the problems with this traditional understanding of ministry is that it demands more than one person can deliver.

This issue came home forcibly to Renee and me when we moved to Santiago, Chile, where we came face-to-face with our limitations and at times total inadequacy. Renee found herself responsible for running an old building near the city center; it had fifty rooms to keep clean and a chapel to maintain. A number of missionaries lived there, plus numerous visitors from the southern part of the country, who were Mapuche Indians who mixed Spanish with their own indigenous language and culture. This complicated communication, especially as we were still learning basic Spanish.

After a couple of years, our regional leader came to our rescue, inviting us to start a new church in a country town that was rapidly becoming a commuting satellite city for the commercial hub and naval port of Valparaiso. We accepted the new challenge eagerly.

We operated out of an old adobe house with a front portion consisting of two rooms, one designated as my office and the other as a recreation room just large enough for table tennis and a central reception area that also served as a chapel. Our bedrooms and kitchen were at the rear.

Before long, we realized that we were facing significant challenges for which my theological training had not prepared me. You see, we had no congregation as yet, apart from one local family that had transferred to us rather than continue to journey into Valparaiso. I tried visiting the neighbors, but a high railing and a fierce dog guarded most homes. The old slogan "a house-visiting pastor makes for a churchgoing population" clearly didn't apply in this situation, and it was becoming less and less valid in the ministry we left in England. It dawned on me that whereas Jesus had trained his intimate group of followers from day one to fish for people, I had been trained to be the curator of an aquarium. And with an empty "tank," I had a lot of time on my hands!

I internalized my sense of failure and anxiety to the extent that I became seriously ill with a bleeding ulcer that confined me to bed for some weeks. As the old saying goes, "Sometimes God lays us on our backs to force us to look up."

During that time I read through the book of Acts to see what I could learn from the experience of the early Christians in their endeavors to start new churches. Eventually I came to the description of Paul's arrival in Corinth, where he was also having a difficult time. Then I read the verse in which the Lord appeared to Paul with the reassuring message, "For I am with you, and no one is going to attack and harm you, because I have many people in this city" (Acts 18:10).

That one verse provided a turning point in my life and ministry in that place. I realized that ministry effectiveness didn't ultimately depend on me but on him. This brought physical healing as I experienced the presence of Christ in a new way. The ulcer cleared up, and I've had no further health problems in that regard since then.

But what about the second part of the Lord's reassurance: "I have many people in this city"? During the following weeks we saw a church come to birth through the most unlikely people. The first appeared at the open window of my office that faced directly onto the sidewalk. I heard a voice say with a heavy Chilean accent, "Hello, my name is Jorge Hansen and I'm Ingleesh." I invited him in, and it soon transpired that what he was really looking for was a job. Finding employment was especially difficult for him because he had a withered arm.

I explained that I had no contacts in the town, but that he had a loving heavenly Father who was concerned for him. He seemed prepared to turn his life over to Jesus so that he could experience that love, so I prayed with and for him that Jesus would meet his need. He was moved by that prayer and invited me to meet his wife and seven-year-old daughter, Angelita— "Little Angel." We became friends and the founding members of our little church.

Now fast-forward thirty-five years. We had supported a missionary family with the South American Missionary Society that was beginning another new church in a city close to the one where we had worked many years before. One day a young Chilean student from that church visited our Anglican church here in Southern California en route to Denver. We were overjoyed to learn that her grandmother was Angelita, who now led the women's work in the church we had started.

The student also updated us on a family that God had brought into our life as his promised "many people in this city." After arriving in that town, we had encountered an ongoing problem with this family, whose back garden faced ours. They persisted in throwing dead animals over the high garden wall, and we threw them back again. They also had two unruly boys who played on their flat roof. On one occasion they dropped some rocks through a glass skylight under which our two small children were playing.

I went straight around the corner to confront the father. He was something of a character in the town; he owned a garage that mended the police jeep and was a heavy drinker. I found him leaning against his house with a bottle of wine in his hand. As I explained what had just happened, he glanced up at the roof to see his two boys still there. His mind was befuddled due to the wine he had consumed, so to placate me he said, "I'll come to your church service one day, Padre." He apparently didn't realize it was Sunday, and I told him I would call for him that evening in time for the worship service.

To fortify his spirit, he consumed even more "refreshment," which resulted in him being rather noisy during the service. At its conclusion, I asked him if he had ever read the Bible. "No," he replied. So I opened one to the book of Proverbs, underlined some verses on disciplining children and gave the Bible to him.

Shortly afterward, a knock came on the door. Standing on the doorstep was the wife of our troublesome neighbor, inquiring what had happened to her old man. She explained that instead of his wine bottle on the meal table, now there was a Bible, and he was reading it. He had evidently moved on from Proverbs.

Some time later he invited his brother along too, as inebriated as he had been on his first visit. When asked why he had brought his brother to church in that state, he replied with a twinkle in his eye, "Oh, he wouldn't have come sober!"

The young Chilean student was able to update us on this family. The man has since died, but his two sons are now grown men actively involved in the church.

One of the problems with anecdotes like these is a tendency to focus on the "evangelism success stories." But far outnumbering the incidents just described are many more stories of disappointment and even of tragedy and scandal. Most of ministry consists of plodding on from day to day and remaining faithful. I'm glad to say that our little church soon passed into the hands of Chilean leaders far more capable at sharing the good news than we were.

LESSONS LEARNED

During our five-year assignment before returning to England, I began to learn some important lessons, which I've had to revisit from time to time. The first is that the Lord Jesus is the one who heads up the church, not me. Second, I'm not God's answer to every challenge and opportunity in the church. He provides others more capable than I in areas such as worship leading, evangelism and long-term pastoral care. It's just as important to recognize where your gifts *don't* lie. I discovered over time that my own giftings are primarily in teaching and encouragement, while Renee's are in compassionate service, hospitality and intercession.

As the pastor of a congregation, my responsibility before God and the people he has placed in my care is to ensure that leadership and mentoring are in place for all of the essential spheres of ministry: apostle, prophet, evangelist, pastor and teacher. However, it's not my responsibility to try to fill every slot. To attempt to do so would result in congregations demanding from me what God had never gifted me to do in the first place.

When I began teaching at Fuller Theological Seminary on church growth, the students wanted to know my qualifications for doing so. I explained frankly that most of what I taught I had learned and continued to learn from people on the frontline actually engaged in church planting. I also added that in Chile I had grown a church fivefold within the space of eighteen months. This impressed them, until I admitted the actual numbers: "We grew from five persons to twenty-five."

HURDLES ASSOCIATED WITH NOMINALISM

Paul's response: Grow up, get connected and become mature persons. In other words, get a life! (See Ephesians 4:14-16.)

In the final section of the passage from Ephesians 4, on which this chapter is based, Paul spoke from the past into our pervasive problem of nominalism. That's a fancy name for people who are Christians in name only. Many who call themselves "Christian" may attend church with greater or lesser frequency, but there is little evidence of their belief impacting their daily life.

Nominality results from failure to address the hurdles identified in the first two categories—individualism and consumerism—which results in Christians becoming stuck at a certain point in increasing self-preoccupation, distraction, disillusionment and marginalization.

A number of years ago, research by the Gallup organization showed that there was no statistically significant difference between churchgoers and non-churchgoers in terms of materialism, truth telling and racism. Only among those who were involved beyond weekly church attendance and were engaged in small groups or ministry teams did significant markers of being Christian became apparent.

Sitting in the pew may provide comfort and preaching, affirming individuals in what they already believe, but that's inadequate to move them forward in their walk with Christ. It's within relational networks that people are transformed through mutual encouragement and correction, learn to respond to each other's needs instead of being self-focused and begin to move out to serve the wider community. That's a model replicated throughout the early churches—all of them small with no place to hide.

What are the hurdles the church faces in regard to its nominal members? Paul identified three, which we can see played out in so many of our churches today.

Hurdle 8: Easily influenced. Like undiscerning children, nominal Christians are easily influenced by those they believe know better than they do. When our children were in their early school years, we experienced their unshakable belief in the infallibility of their teachers. "But Miss So-and-So says . . ." was the predictable response to any alternative opinion. Sometimes this carries over into adulthood in the church. We buy the latest spiritual speculations as though they were irrefutable facts. Ignorance and instability characterizes young children as well as immature believers, who are easily influenced and can therefore be exploited through their misplaced trust. Both the Old and the New Testaments warn us against false shepherds who, through their influence on church leaders, lead their flocks astray.

Hurdle 9: Tossed to and fro. Paul also likened immature believers to a boat tossed to and fro, entirely at the mercy of wind and waves (Ephesians 4:14). Once a boat has lost steerage, it is whirled about, and once it turns broadside to the next big wave, it's likely to capsize and sink. On such a craft you don't know whether you are coming or going; you lose any sense of direction as your boat is tossed by every wind and carried along by every current. Distressed sailors grab at any life raft floated to them. In SOS situations, many nominal Christians look for one quick fix after another. This confused state of affairs is compounded, spreading throughout the congregation when the leaders themselves lose their sense of direction and fail to provide guidance to the church.

Hurdle 10: Vulnerable to predators. There is no shortage of religious scam artists in our day, just as there was no shortage in Paul's. These are unscrupulous individuals who through their dark arts and deceptive schemes make money off desperate people and those who buy into a health, wealth and prosperity package, or they seek to gain control over them by their demands. Their presence creates a toxic environment resulting from unrealized expectations, exploitation of the vulnerable and cynicism on the part of those who see through deceptive practices.

LIMITATIONS OF THE HURDLING IMAGE

Throughout this chapter we have used the image of hurdling, yet we must recognize that any image has its limitations. In the first place, it's not intended as a competitive model. Individuals and churches are not to compare their performance against those running in the same race. Also, unlike the hurdles on the running track, the church's hurdles are not identical or spaced evenly. We are there to assist one another when a particular hurdle seems insurmountable. The objective is not to win the race, but to complete the course, with the encouragement of others and giving others our support.

Paul's response to the dangers of nominality was to encourage Christians to mature by "[growing] up into him who is the Head" (Ephesians 4:15). But Christians don't mature like wines or cheeses, kept in a controlled and safe environment for a specified period. Jesus demonstrated in the training of his disciples that maturity comes through exposure to the pressures, opportunities and challenges of living out our faith in a world that constantly questions and challenges the vision of God's kingdom with its alternative scenarios.

Maturity signifies growth that is comprehensive and holistic—not selective. How are we to leave nominalism and become mature? Not simply by saying the right things, but by embodying the truth we proclaim. Paul didn't actually say "speaking the truth in love," but literally "truthing in love." In his commentary on this passage, John Stott wrote, "Truth becomes hard if it is not softened by love; love becomes soft if it is not strengthened by truth."

Paul did not confine his exhortation to a religious elite. His pleas for unity in the body of Christ were "to prepare God's people for works of service, so that the body of Christ may be built up until *we all* reach unity in the faith and in the knowledge of the Son of God and become mature, attaining to the whole measure of the fullness of Christ" (Ephesians 4:12-13, emphasis added). Because a body is made up of many different members, unity is not mind-numbing, predictable uniformity, but complex interconnectedness within amazing variety.

MOTIVATION FOR OVERCOMING PERSONAL HURDLES

During my National Service in the Royal Air Force, I was posted to a base in a remote area of eastern England. I had just become engaged to Renee, and with no car and no local rail service, it was impossible to get home on weekends unless I could get a ride from a friend with a car.

One day I saw a notice that announced the annual RAF cross-country race. I confess that I'm no great athlete, but this event was scheduled close to Nottingham, our hometown. I suddenly gained an interest in cross-country running, so I signed up to represent my base. For the next few weeks I ran around the base in an endeavor to get fit. I was okay on short distances, but long distances presented a challenge.

The day of the race came around, and a bus stopped at each

base in the area to pick up competitors. On arrival at the RAF base near Nottingham, all the runners assembled in the gymnasium, where the physical training instructor announced that the course was a challenging one. We would leave the road after a short while and then run over plowed fields, through long grass, over fences, through hedgerows, across ditches, through muddy patches and over hills. "If you're fit, you can make it," he said. "If you aren't, you shouldn't be here."

I set out among 140 runners and was gradually overtaken by those who were fitter than I. But I kept going, with the encouragement of others who were also struggling, and made it to the end, finishing in 104th place.

I learned two valuable lessons from that experience. First, with strong enough motivation you can find the stamina and determination to keep going to the bitter end. Second, make sure you have the right motivation; otherwise you will end up disappointed. You see, I never did meet up with my fiancée, because immediately after the cross-country event we were loaded into buses and returned to camp.

We must be prepared to encounter any or all of the hurdles identified in this chapter. They may challenge us as individuals, as a group or at the congregational level. For the church to tackle the three categories of hurdles—individualism, consumerism and nominalism—it must depend on building supportive relationships, rather than on individualistic, spiritual-fitness exercise programs.

QUESTIONS FOR THOUGHT AND DISCUSSION

1. Identify the hurdles your group has encountered and the ways in which you have dealt with each. How do they affect

you personally? How do they affect the circle of Christians with whom you fellowship?

2. How has our cultural bias toward individualism weakened our relationship with family and friends? In what ways are your friendships self-serving and manipulative? In what ways do you have genuine concern for the well-being of the other person? Do you ever undervalue or put down other people?

3. In your church or group, are there appeals for volunteers that go unheeded or that the same few people respond to every time? What evidence is there that individuals and groups are coming up with ideas and taking initiative? How can the leaders of your church create a climate that encourages creative thinking and risk-taking?

4. What percentage of the regular attendees are involved in ministry in accordance with their gifts, either within the church or by the church in its service in the community and beyond? In what ways are individuals helped to identify and develop their gifts and passion for ministry?

5. In the early years of the church, each congregation identified those members who had the gift and passion to communicate the good news, and the faith community surrounded them in reinforcing the message with their witness and their acts of service to the community. In what ways can your faith community support the use of gifts?

6. How well equipped is your church or group to discern teaching that is faithful to the Scriptures and to the historic creeds of the church? In what ways is it vulnerable to false teaching and to being tossed to and fro by the latest theories or speculations?

3

DYING

A FRUITFUL WAY TO LIVE

I have been crucified with Christ and I no longer live,
but Christ lives in me. The life I live in the body, I live by faith
in the Son of God, who loved me and gave himself for me.

GALATIANS 2:20

This picture stands in stark, and even shocking, contrast to the chapter's subtitle. This monumental sculpture of Christ being nailed to the cross is by Chris Slatoff, artist in residence at the Brehm Center for Worship, Theology and the Arts at

Fuller Theological Seminary. As an adjunct professor, he inspires many students to give expression to their artistic talent.
The work serves as a constant reminder to students, as they
walk by it each day, of the price Jesus himself paid for our salvation and of the cost entailed in following him, which we explore in this chapter.

COMING TO TERMS WITH DEATH AND DYING

The West is a death-denying culture. We find death incredibly
difficult to face, and when it happens, we often don't handle it
well. We have few healthy processes for grieving; this was especially the case with my parents' generation. After the funeral,
the dead person was hardly mentioned. And when he or she
was discussed, it was with platitudes or with lighthearted anecdotes to conceal one's real feelings. Even the person's photos
were removed from display.

There is an underlying though usually unmentioned dread of
death because for the majority of the population there is no
hope beyond the grave. This sense of finality is more prevalent
in Europe than in North America. Especially among the more
"stiff upper lip" northern Europeans, the deceased relative is
usually visited briefly at the funeral home, but then the casket is
closed. In contrast, during funeral services in Eastern Orthodox
and ethnic churches, there is an open casket for mourners to
pay their respects—and even to touch or kiss their loved one.

Every culture has its own rituals. Where death occurs in a
domestic setting and where more people die young or suffer
lingering deaths without the benefit of modern drugs, death is
more readily observable and close at hand.

Every human family, no matter how much it tries to avoid
the subject and live in denial, has to face the issue of death.
Sometimes it comes to an elderly person at the end of a fulfilled

life, and the living can celebrate. Such funerals and memorial services can indeed be joyful, and even triumphant, occasions. At other times, when a baby, child or young person is taken, we are left in anguish and with unanswered questions. This issue became very personal for us when Renee and I were expecting a new baby. All went well until the final weeks of the pregnancy, when the doctor realized that something was seriously wrong. The baby was no longer moving and positioning herself as she should. By the time Renee went into the hospital, she knew that the baby had died in her womb. She was placed in a ward full of expectant mothers with the knowledge that her baby would not enter this world alive. It was a time of drawing strength from the Lord, and she took great comfort from the Psalms, underlining in the Bible she still uses today.

The hospital asked if we wanted to see our baby girl. We both held her briefly in our arms and named her Alison. For us that was an important moment of closure, but *closure* is not the right word. We were handing her back to the Lord for his safekeeping.

It is not only families that have to face death, but also the family of God. We face the death of individuals at every stage of life within the congregation. Again, some funerals are times of joyful celebration of elderly saints. At other times the situation is heart wrenching. We need the reminder that the church as "the communion of saints" consists not just of the church militant here on earth but also of the church triumphant in heaven. We need to live in anticipation of joining that "great multitude that no one could count, from every nation, tribe, people and language, standing before the throne and in front of the Lamb" (Revelation 7:9). The lamb is Christ himself, who laid down his life as a sacrifice for the sins of the world.

WHY CHURCHES DIE

It's not only individuals within congregations but churches themselves that need to learn to die with dignity. Some churches die because they have for so long resisted the grace of Christ and have lived more in denial of the power of the gospel than as communities that demonstrate its power to transform lives and beneficially impact wider society. Other churches die because the community they served disperses. Still others die as a result of the persistent onslaught of persecution. So many of the churches mentioned in the New Testament are no longer in existence today or are a shadow of their former selves. What happened to the vibrant Christian centers of learning in North Africa and the Middle East, where today Islam holds sway? We still live with the tragic legacy of the Crusades of the Middle Ages.

No one can guarantee the future of any church. This throwaway line is all too true: "Every church is just one generation away from extinction." Some churches can't survive, because they are not prepared to die to their outworn traditions and self-focused agendas. The members simply cling together, sustained by their shared memories, with the attitude "the last one out, please turn out the lights."

DYING IN ORDER TO LIVE

Why talk about the death of the physical body at the beginning of this chapter? And why place a chapter on death near the beginning of a book instead of where we normally assume dying to belong: at the end? Because, for anyone following Christ, dying to self is an essential part of life.

If we haven't learned to die in the *midst* of life, it will be all the harder at the *end* of our life. In stating this, I'm not speaking of near-death experiences or of surviving life-threatening diseases—although some of us who have faced such traumatic experiences or are in the midst of an anxiety-producing prognosis even now may readily identify with our theme. Rather I'm speaking of any time in life when it seems that we have hit a wall in terms of our future. Our hopes have been dashed, and a seeming abyss lies before us.

I've attended many leadership seminars over the years in which instructors encouraged us to set out our life goals and to map out our future step-by-step in order to achieve them. I smile to myself, because that isn't how life has panned out for me. But then, God deals with each of us in different ways, according to our personality, our cultural context, our circumstances, and our need for inner transformation and for developing new competencies at the appropriate time.

In Renee's and my journey—both as individuals and as a couple—each new chapter has come as a surprise to us. And each entailed a "dying."

After working in industry for two years, followed by two years of compulsory military service, I went off to seminary for five long years. Renee and I married in my final year. Then we served a two-year curacy (assistant pastorate) in an Anglican parish in South London, believing that we would remain in parish ministry in England with a call to the inner city. But God had other plans. We had to let go of our vision for the future and head off to South America—without the benefit of one day's missionary training or language school.

In Chile we soon found we had to die to much of what we'd learned from our ministry training and experience in England, and we had to learn afresh from our new Chilean friends. We were assigned to be with a team of fellow missionaries beginning new churches in urban centers, but we had never had the benefit of a course to teach us how to do that.

After five years, we were unexpectedly called back to the United Kingdom for me to serve as the home and education secretary for our mission. There I was frequently invited to speak on the growth of the church in South America. After one such meeting, I was asked to write a twenty-eight-page booklet in the Grove Series, published at that time by St. John's College, Nottingham. My assigned title was "Urban Church Growth, Clues from South America." Due to that brief contribution, I became "Mr. Church Growth," which indicates just how desperate church leaders were in the mid-1970s and 1980s.

To make a long story short, I need to add briefly two further experiences of dying. The first was during the next seven years, when I was working with the Bible Society in England, Wales and Northern Ireland under its visionary leader, Tom Houston. Part of my job entailed conducting seminars for church leaders on the use of the Bible in the renewal of the church through discipleship and mission. Demand became so great that I was neglecting my publishing and area staff responsibilities, so I hired a Baptist pastor as a colleague to further develop and run the seminars. In other words, I had to give away that part of the job I loved the most. I had to die again by giving back to God the very ministry I believed he had entrusted to me.

But I've discovered that when God brings about a dying process, it leads to resurrection. Unknown to me, God was releasing me from my previous responsibilities so that I could be on loan from the Bible Society to serve as the national training director for Mission England, a two-year program that came to a climax with six Billy Graham Missions around Britain.

The saga continues. Early in my appointment in the Bible Society, I was sent to Fuller to sit in on a two-week intensive course. Through the generosity of the Bible Society and the flexibility of the seminary, this led to the completion of my degree. I began as a "provisional, probationary student" and ended up being invited to join the faculty. And I said yes. I'm sure that Fuller didn't fully realize the risk it was taking. At first it was very intimidating to be surrounded by scholars who had dedicated their lives to their particular area of expertise. And in my heart of hearts, I knew I was not an academic, so once again I had to learn to die—this time in the midst of my work.

LIVING THROUGH THE LEARNING CURVE

In business literature on leadership, we are cautioned by the Peter Principle, which states, "People tend to be promoted to their level of incompetence." We can easily end up with a mismatch between our prior experiences and the management and leadership position we find ourselves occupying. For those in spiritual leadership, this is a sure sign that we have stepped outside the will of God. We may have been driven by an inflated ego rather than by a sense of God's call. Or perhaps we were simply impetuous, and our impatience caused us to arrive too soon.

At the age of forty-seven, when I first arrived at Fuller, what you saw was what you got. For the first time I had to learn to stop emulating other people and to be myself. I've spent the past twenty-five years learning so much from my colleagues as I've interpreted their knowledge through my own experience and shared it in North America and around the world.

Now, in my seventies and after fifty years of ordained ministry and teaching, I've had to die once more as I struggle to interpret a rapidly changing world. I'm on the greatest learning curve of my entire career, and many students and younger church leaders have become my teachers. They understand far better than my

generation, and even many boomers, how to do ministry in the
noncontrolling, networking environment that permeates our
culture. (We will explore this theme in chapter five.)

This is my story, and it's different for each of us. I encourage
you to look back over the years to identify the dying that you
have had to undergo. Think of your past life in terms of
chapters rather than years. As one chapter ended and the next
opened up, was there at the same time a dying and a rebirth
taking place?

During times of traumatic transition, don't get stuck in resentment. In the hands of the risen Lord, dying is always accompanied by resurrection. Also stand alongside individuals in
your immediate family in their dying processes, providing
guidance and encouragement. And help the church community
through a similar process.

THE DANGER OF LIVING IN DENIAL

During the journey Jesus made with his disciples from Galilee to
Jerusalem, on two occasions he attempted to prepare them for
what would happen within a few days of their arrival (see Mark
8:31-38; 10:32-34). Matthew and Luke also recorded this important lesson (see Matthew 16:21-28; Luke 9:22-27). He would
be "rejected by the elders, chief priests and teachers of the law,"
in other words the entire religious establishment, "and . . . he
must be killed and after three days rise again" (Mark 8:32). If only
they had paid attention, they would have been spared so much
disillusionment, misunderstanding and feelings of abandonment.

On each of the occasions recorded by Mark in his Gospel,
the disciples failed to comprehend. Their minds were so filled
with the anticipated triumph of the Messiah declaring himself
in Jerusalem and with what that might signify for them, his
closest followers. They could not conceive of a rejected Messiah

who would suffer and die. Just like those disciples, we too can become deaf to what we don't want to hear or to what flies in the face of what we eagerly anticipate.

THE SIGNIFICANCE OF JESUS' OWN DEATH

"The hour has come for the Son of Man to be glorified. Very truly, I tell you, unless a grain of wheat falls into the earth and dies, it remains just a single grain; but if it dies, it bears much fruit" (John 12:23-24 NRSV). This statement contains two monumental surprises.

The first surprise is that Jesus refers to his crucifixion as the hour for the Son of Man to be glorified, though the cross was a symbol of excruciating suffering and public shame. For Jesus, his death on the cross was in order to fulfill the mission of his heavenly Father to die for the sins of the world. It was not his moment of disgrace, but the hour of his Father's glory. His vindication would not be long in coming, when three days later his tomb was found empty. His body had not been stolen, but had been raised by the power of the Holy Spirit. The early church could declare triumphantly, "The Lord is risen!" and is now ascended into heaven.

The second monumental surprise is that Jesus regarded his death not in terms of termination but of germination. He likened his death to a single seed that falls into the ground, not just to produce "many seeds." That phrase is more accurately translated in the New Revised Standard Version as "bears much fruit" (John 12:24)—fruit that is the life of Jesus evident in the lives of countless people in all cultures around the world who have submitted their lives to him and received the gift of his Holy Spirit.

To appreciate the deeper significance of Jesus' statement, we need to put his words into context. Certain Greeks were among the non-Jews who had come to Jerusalem for the Passover. Philip passed on a message from them to Jesus: they wanted an opportunity to see him up close, in person. They were there because they were attracted to the Jewish faith, but still felt like outsiders—and were treated that way.

On this occasion they felt even more alien because of the extraordinary event they had just witnessed—Jesus riding into Jerusalem and the crowds giving him a royal welcome, quite literally, by shouting, "Hosanna! Blessed is he who comes in the name of the Lord! Blessed is the King of Israel!" (John 12:13). In the midst of such nationalistic fervor, they likely felt out of it, so they wanted to see Jesus to get some answers.

At first sight it may seem that Jesus simply ignored their request. But in the long term they got much more than just a brief interview. There was a great deal more at stake. Their initiative is associated with the hour having come for the Son of Man to be glorified. The key to understand the significance of this passage is in his response: "'And I, when I am lifted up from the earth, will draw all people to myself.' He said this to show the kind of death he was going to die" (John 12:32-33 NIV 2011).

The Greeks' desire to see Jesus at the moment when he was reaching the climax of his mission was premature. After his death, rising and ascension, Jesus himself would be reaching out to them—not for a brief interview, but that he might be among them in a life-transforming way. Their simple request would eventually be answered beyond their wildest dreams.

We need the constant reminder that it's the crucified and risen Christ who draws people to himself and not just the impressive testimony or persuasive message of evangelists. We have a significant role to play, but we are never the key player. We simply deliver the invitation. It's the Holy Spirit, at work in the heart of the seeker or in turning around the cynic, who is the principal agent. Still more, the risen Christ can reveal himself without any human agencies. There are countless stories told by credible witnesses of individuals encountering Christ through visions, dreams and miraculous interventions on their behalf.

FOLLOWING CHRIST ENTAILS CARRYING THE CROSS

Jesus warns us of the high cost of following him—a warning we Western Christians need to heed. Our insistence on a gospel that meets our every need without significantly challenging our priorities or redirecting our lives results in our having little understanding of the place of suffering, self-denial and even death in identifying with Christ.

Jesus made this abundantly clear to his first disciples, as he does to us today: "Whoever wants to be my disciple must deny themselves and take up their cross and follow me. For whoever wants to save their life will lose it, but whoever loses their life for me will find it. What good will it be for someone to gain the whole world, yet forfeit their soul? Or what can anyone give in exchange for their soul?" (Matthew 16:24-26 NIV 2011).

Although the disciples were reluctant to heed his warnings, because their minds were elsewhere, it's clear from the account of the early church and the letters of the New Testament that suffering and dying for Christ played an increasingly prominent part in their understanding of the cost of following him. Some early Christians literally died physically for their faith, and many others suffered the same fate during the subsequent persecutions by Roman emperors. Throughout the following centuries, many more have suffered martyrdom and continue to do so to this day.

Baptism was a big step for anyone to take in the early church, as it is now for new believers who face family opposition or a society set on persecuting the church. Consequently, baptism signifies more than a cleansing from sin; it also entails a dying to the old way of life: "For we know that our old self was crucified with him so that the body of sin might be done away with, that we should no longer be slaves to sin—because anyone who has died has been freed from sin" (Romans 6:6-7). Faced with such a challenging statement, we must admit that all of us have a great deal of dying still to do.

This same passage reminds us not only of the saving *death* of Christ but also of his saving *life*. Paul already stated in the previous verse: "If we have been united with him like this in his death, we will certainly also be united with him in his resurrection." This statement is then followed by, "Now if we died with Christ, we believe that we will also live with him" (verses 5, 8). The theme of dying to live runs right through Paul's letters.

Christians want to experience the power of Christ's resurrection, but there is a condition, which Paul spelled out in personal terms when he declared, "I want to know Christ and the power of his resurrection and the fellowship of sharing in his sufferings, becoming like him in his death, and so, somehow, to attain to the resurrection from the dead" (Philippians 3:10-11).

One of my greatest privileges during the past thirty years has been to meet with Christians from all walks of life in many different parts of the world. I love to sit one-on-one or in small groups and listen to their stories. I'm reminded of a Russian Christian in Moscow who had to move from one university to another—three in all—when the Marxist authorities refused to grant him his degree because of his Christian faith. Eventually he was permitted to graduate but then placed in a mental institution to curtail his ministry. He told me this story without a hint of resentment.

I also have heard the stories of older Christian Armenians whose grandparents were massacred during the Turkish atrocities. And I've visited churches in Korea, joining in their prayer vigils and hearing their stories of God's provision in the midst of the suffering they experienced during the Japanese occupation and the Korean War. I've talked with young former drug addicts in the United Kingdom and here in the United States who found freedom in Christ from their addiction. And with students at Fuller, where I was privileged to teach, hearing stories of broken lives mended and turned around. Jesus' promise is being fulfilled to this day around the world. As he said, "I . . . will draw all people to myself" (John 12:32 NIV 2011).

CHRISTIANS CAN'T EXPECT IMMUNITY FROM TRAGEDY AND SUFFERING

Christians live in an out-of-kilter world due to human rebellion dating back to Adam and Eve. It's a world of violence, suffering, injustice and death. And believers are not immune from the consequences of human rebellion in general and of their own acts of compromise and disobedience. Furthermore, our suffering may not result from our own misdeeds, but may simply be the fallout from living in a fallen world.

In the midst of his chronic suffering, Paul reassured the Christians in Corinth with a word he himself received from the ascended Lord: "'My grace is sufficient for you, for my power is made perfect in weakness.' Therefore I will boast all the more gladly about my weaknesses, so that Christ's power may rest on me. That is why, for Christ's sake, I delight in weaknesses, in insults, in hardships, in persecutions, in difficulties. For when I am weak, then I am strong" (2 Corinthians 12:8-10).

WHAT TO DO WHEN YOU HIT ROCK BOTTOM

Jesus' story of the prodigal son presents us with a case study of a young man who in his boredom, restlessness and rebellion decided to demand his share of his inheritance from his father. In doing so he not only rejected his father but treated him as already dead (see Luke 15:11-32).

The headstrong, rebellious young man wandered into a far country, living it up for as long as his resources lasted. Then his "friends," who were simply taking advantage of him, deserted him. He ended up doing a job that no person of his race would contemplate: he cleaned out pigsties and even ate their slop. When he realized that he had hit rock bottom, he knew his only recourse was to return home. But how could he face the father he had grieved and wronged, and what about his self-righteous older brother, who may have been part of his problem in the first place? Rebelliousness, greed, jealousy and resentment are powerful adversaries.

During the long and arduous journey home, begging as he went, with his once fine clothes now reduced to filthy rags, he rehearsed what he was going to say to his father. He wondered if he would be rejected out of hand and his elder brother would treat him with the contempt he deserved.

But his father had been waiting with eager anticipation for his return. He had kept one eye on the task at hand and the other always looking into the distance for the first sign of his son. When the longed-for day arrived, he recognized his son in the distance, despite the young man's tragically altered appearance. The father ran to meet him and embraced him. He put new robes on him and organized a celebratory feast. The only one who refused to attend the party was the elder son.

Some Bible commentators have speculated on what might have happened if the elder son had intercepted the returning prodigal before the father's welcome. It doesn't bear thinking about. Tragically, some churches resemble the elder son rather than reflect the compassion of the grieving father.

Consider another biblical story. When we are faced with an overwhelming tragedy or when tragedy comes hard on the heels of previous tragedies from which we have not had time to recover, how are we to respond? That was the plight of Job, who suffered the loss of everything. It began when invaders carried off his oxen. Next, a lightning strike killed his sheep and all but one of his shepherds. Then Chaldean raiders stole his camels and killed all his servants. Then his house collapsed, blasted by a powerful wind, killing all his children. Finally his health broke down, and he was covered in boils.

At this point his three "comforters" arrived to offer explanations and to identify the source of his woes. They were convinced that Job must have brought the suffering on himself. The arguments go back and forth throughout the book. Their counsel was theologically orthodox but utterly irrelevant and misdirected. Their arguments simply added to Job's misery rather than providing enlightenment and comfort.

I remember the day I received a phone call from the attorney of a distressed family. He explained that parents living nearby had just lost their two-year-old daughter, drowned in the swimming pool in their backyard. The attorney had found the number of our church in the phone book and asked me if I would call at their home. I arrived as a complete stranger, unannounced, and explained to the distraught father that I was the associate rector of a local Anglican church.

He immediately took me upstairs where his wife lay weeping with photos of their two-year-old spread on the bed. We simply spent the evening crying together, while they told me about the child that had been snatched from them. It was not the time for fumbled explanations. How could one even begin to make sense of such a tragedy?

But after that night and over the past decade, our friendship has developed. It has been a long and painful journey, but one of increasing joy and comfort, with the gradual emergence of faith and hope. On the human level, ours is an unlikely friendship in that we have so little in common. They are pop musicians, and we are an elderly couple that has never been to a pop concert. Yet tragedy brought our hearts together. Our sharing is at a much deeper level than mutual interest could ever take us.

DISOBEDIENCE IS A FUTILE DOWNHILL JOURNEY

The story of Jonah reads like a comic strip; it's visual and dramatic. Jonah was a reluctant prophet who, when called by God to go to "the great city Nineveh," the capital of Israel's longtime enemy, set off in the opposite direction. He was determined to place as much distance between himself and God's intended destination.

His disobedience was a downhill journey every step of the way; it demonstrates the utter futility of trying to flee from the Lord when he asks us to die to ourselves by doing what he asks. Jonah headed for the port of Tarshish (probably located in either eastern Spain or western Turkey), the edge of the world as far as Jonah was concerned. He went *down* to Joppa, "where he found a ship bound for that port" (Jonah 1:3). (Note that it's a mistake to assume that every simple solution and ready connection like this one is a sign of God's approval. Beware of convenient "ships" that may sail you away from God's calling.)

During the voyage, Jonah went down into his cabin to seek refuge in the midst of a fierce storm. He, the prophet, slept while the pagan sailors on deck prayed to their gods as they battled the storm that threatened to break up the ship. The sailors believed that their plight was caused by the displeasure of their gods. But who was the culprit? None other than Jonah. Once identified, Jonah admitted his fault and asked the sailors to throw him into the raging waters as the only way of saving themselves and their vessel. So he continued his downward journey into the depths of the ocean. He cried out to the Lord, "From the depths of the grave I called for help. . . . To the roots of the mountains I sank down" (Jonah 2:2, 6). God provided him a means of protection and deliverance in the form of the big fish that swallowed him. In that dark and smelly prayer chamber, Jonah knew that his prayer had been heard by God in his holy temple. Yet this was not to be his lowest point. That comes later in the story.

Jonah eventually arrived in Nineveh, where he faithfully declared God's message of judgment. After all, judgment was what Israel demanded of their God. Once Nineveh was destroyed, Jonah could then return home as a national hero for his boldness in declaring God's message in the very streets of "the great city of Nineveh." But it didn't turn out as Jonah had anticipated. The city repented and was spared—at least for the time being.

This brings us to Jonah's lowest moment, with his lonely but futile vantage point overlooking the city. We find him complaining to God and revealing the real reason for his disobedience: "O LORD, is this not what I said when I was still at home? That is why I was so quick to flee to Tarshish. I knew that you are a gracious and compassionate God, slow to anger and abounding in love, a God who relents from sending calamity. Now, O LORD, take away my life, for it is better for me to die than to live" (Jonah 4:2-3).

The story concludes with Jonah as a pathetic figure, more concerned about the fact that the shady vine provided by God had perished, leaving him exposed to the hot sun, than about the fate of the 120,000 inhabitants of the city. Jonah's concern for the city fell pathetically short of God's.

Jonah's behavior and its results provide a stinging critique of Israel's lack of concern for the nation it considered its enemy. It comes with equal force to challenge those churches today that persist with Jonah's judgmental detachment. Before we pray for the growth of our church, we have to ask ourselves in all honesty, "Does God want more churches like ours?" Or do they need to die to be reborn as places of grace, mercy and hospitality?

FRUITFULNESS ENTAILS PAINFUL PRUNING

Renee is an ardent gardener. Her specialty is roses, which she has cultivated in both England and California. Each autumn I watch her not only cut off the dead flowers but also drastically, to my way of thinking, cut back the branches. We also live close to Napa Valley, California, a wine-growing area. Here too the treatment meted out seems drastic. However, without such cutting back, both rosebushes and grapevines would become overgrown, and the result would be poor-quality flowers and grapes.

Jesus declared to his disciples during his intimate conversations in the upper room in the hours before his crucifixion that he is "the true vine" (John 15:1). The imagery is not lost on his disciples, because the picture of Israel as the vineyard and the vine is familiar to them from the Hebrew Scriptures. Those same passages also warn Israel that, in rejecting him, the vineyard has lost its protective walls, and in place of the vine of God's planting, wild vines have intruded. The nation's spiritual and political leaders have neglected their responsibilities. So Jesus as Messiah comes to replace a neglected vineyard as its true vine.

His disciples were given the responsibility of caring for his people, which entails two requirements: first, to abide in Christ, and second, to be prepared to submit to his pruning. *If* occurs

five times in this passage as a caution that we have to participate actively in the life of the vine, for we can become easily
distracted and preoccupied with other interests and concerns.
Abiding (the word used in the NASB) must be distinguished
from *hiding*. It does not signify the avoidance of responsibility.
It's not an invitation to become cowardly or lazy. It signifies a
relationship rather than a *refuge*, meaning yielding to Christ's
control and drawing our very life and sustenance from him.
For Jesus' disciples, *abiding* meant developing an already existing relationship. The same applies to believers today. But
some of us may still need to take the initial step in coming to
Christ. Having come, we all then need to learn to remain in him
and not to attempt to go it alone, for that results only in disaster.

When Jesus stated that we can do nothing apart from him,
he was not implying that we are rendered utterly helpless if we
choose to ignore him and live an independent life. We may
have profound spiritual insights and be able to live according to
a high moral code, but no one can live a Christlike life unless
he or she abides in him.

Abiding has a cozy ring to it, but Jesus' second point dispels
that image. Abiding not only requires patience, it also entails
pain. Jesus wants us to *be* better and to *do* better. The disciples
gathered in the upper room were already in the process of being
pruned. Jesus' word picture of "pruning" can also be translated
clean or *pure*. But it's a continuing process, and they still had a
long way to go.

Jesus is not content to leave us as we are; he is determined to
trim the excess from our lives. Pruning is a drastic and painful
process that involves death. Consequently, the amateur gardener tends to prune timidly for fear of damaging or killing off
the plant. But the skillful professional is prepared to cut back
huge amounts. It's a drastic process that can appear to be very

cruel. God may use pain, sorrow, disappointment or frustrated and misdirected ambition to prune us—paring us back to essentials and cutting out our dead wood. His objective is to increase not foliage but fruit. The Lord is not being destructive, yet there is a price to pay in order to become more productive. The purpose of pruning is greater fruitfulness: "more fruitful . . . much fruit" John 15:2, 5, 8). But right after the gardener's pruning, it appears that fruitfulness is impossible. It's the same way after God's pruning. But we believe through faith and experience that we will bear fruit.

When Jesus says, "Abide in me," he isn't asking us to stay and be pruned to the point that there's nothing left. In his hands the pruning always leads to fruitfulness, provided we learn to submit to it. But what happens when the pruning ends in death? There is the supreme test of faith. As Christians, we believe that life on this planet is an inconclusive experience. Our years here are but the preface to the fuller life. *Fruitful* living is a far more worthwhile lifetime goal than *successful* living.

The two questions that all servants of Christ need to ask themselves are: "What do I want to be known for at the end of my life?" and "How can I finish well?" The secret of finishing well is to abide in Christ and to submit to his pruning, no matter how painful. Fruitfulness is not the result of what we do, but the outcome of who we are.

OUR LIFE HERE IS A PRELUDE TO ETERNAL LIFE

In our culture we place great emphasis on living well, but dying well is equally important. Some end-of-life scenarios are deeply distressing, with great pain caused by a degenerative condition that gradually results in the weakening and failure of vital organs. Yet, in the midst of suffering, we can see the grace of God at work in powerful and unanticipated ways.

Returning home one evening from the church, I found a phone message with a man's voice asking me to contact him. On returning the man's call, I was surprised to hear a woman scarcely able to speak through her tears. I apologized for phoning at an inappropriate moment, but explained that I had received a request to do so. She replied, "That was my brother on my behalf, but I would like to speak with you."

She went on to explain the reason for her distress. She was dying of pancreatic cancer; the oncologist had given her just two weeks to live. "I am, or rather was, a professional dancer," she said. "And I was watching a video of myself dancing when you called. I guess it just got to me as I lay here in bed scarcely able to move, doped with morphine." I asked if it would be appropriate for me to visit her, and she said she would like that very much.

The next day I visited her home and found her lying in bed, hooked up to her morphine drip. In the course of our conversation, she shared her two major concerns: she felt increasingly lonely and she felt utterly helpless. Even in her condition, she still possessed an outgoing personality, which I suppose is typical of many theater folks. "I have always gained great satisfaction from doing things for people," she said. "And now I can do nothing."

We chatted for some time over the issue of an increased sense of loneliness. Such alienation is distressingly aggravated in families I've visited in which both the dying person and the immediate family know that the end is drawing near but the subject is studiously avoided. Fortunately, this was not the situation for her.

We eventually came to a point in the conversation when I was able to say, "Your increasing feeling of being alone is inevitable. You know that no matter how sympathetic and loving

your visitors are, they don't really understand what it's like to
face imminent death. For the vast majority, it is a once-in-a-
lifetime experience. But try to look at it not as separation *from*
but as separation *for.*"

As I asked God how I could most appropriately share the
good news of Jesus with this sensitive and vulnerable woman,
who was not a churchgoer and was more focused on New Age
philosophy and health foods, these words of Jesus to his disciples just before his own death popped into my mind, and I
spoke them: "In my Father's house are many rooms; if it were
not so, I would have told you. I am going there to prepare a
place for you. And if I go and prepare a place for you, I will
come back and take you to be with me that you also may be
where I am" (John 14:2-3).

She looked at me in amazement. "I know those words. My
father was the conductor of a symphony orchestra and composed an oratorio on John's Gospel. One of the solos dwelt on
those assuring words." From that single passage, I did my best
to make clear how Jesus is uniquely qualified to give that as-
surance on the authority of his heavenly Father. We talked about
the journey from alienation to reconciliation. I felt that the Holy
Spirit had reached into the depths of her soul, and we prayed a
prayer of commitment. I was then able to add the words that
Jesus spoke to his disciples so that she could be assured: "You
know the way to the place where I am going" (see John 14:4).

In response to her second concern—the feeling of help-
lessness—with some trepidation, I ventured: "This might seem
strange, but there is one very important thing that you can do
for your circle of friends, family and neighbors."

"And what is that?" she asked.

"Would you share your dying with us, because that is something we all have to face eventually?"

At some point in that conversation, her oncologist made a house call to check on her treatment and condition, during which I stepped out of the room. He popped his head around the door and said, "You had better go back in." By that time she was too tired and medicated for further conversation. So I bid her goodbye, and on the way out I said, "You know your dancing days are not over. They have just begun!"

And she did share her new life during those two weeks before she died. My wife and I were privileged to lead in a very simple memorial service held in her home, which was attended by many of her friends from the entertainment world. They each spoke in turn, saying that they had received a call from her during the past few days and what an impact her final words of faith and peace had made.

Among those in the circle was an elderly woman in a wheel-chair—her mother. My dying friend had informed me that she spoke daily with her mother on the phone, but they could not meet face-to-face because her mother was in an advanced stage of renal failure. She gave me her number, which led to a visit. I took with me a tiny Communion set that had been given to me when my wife and I went to Chile to serve the Anglican church there. As I placed the bread on the little silver plate and poured wine into the cup, I told her the story of how I had come to have these items. "Well, I never," she exclaimed. "For a time my husband was guest conductor with the Chilean Philharmonic through the American Cultural Institute."

We found her that day in bed in a fetal position. Her son, who had first called me about his sister, was present on that occasion and said that she never left the house. But at her daughter's memorial service, there she sat in her wheelchair.

Whatever level of performance we have managed on the dance floor, or if we have never dared or cared to step onto one, we all need the reminder when our call comes that our dancing days aren't over but have just begun.

Suffering and dying followed by resurrection is a pattern of life for individuals, families and churches. Coming to Christ is not a smooth transition. It's not simply an "add on" to what we are already doing. Dying is also the rhythm of ministry in the church. It requires our being prepared to let go of so much trash and baggage in order to rediscover the treasure of the gospel. There is no escaping the need to undergo painful pruning and dying in order that we might experience more fully the resurrection life. Also, for the church to keep living, it needs to die to its concern for self-preservation and live to fulfill Christ's mission in the world.

QUESTIONS FOR THOUGHT AND DISCUSSION

1. Recall the things people have said to you about death, from those who regard death as final with no hope beyond the grave, to those who believe that we are transformed into angels, to those who believe in reincarnation, to those who believe that life on earth is a prelude to life in eternity, to those who avoid the topic altogether. How does the death, resurrection and ascension of Jesus give the Christian a sure and certain hope (see Hebrews 11:1)?

2. Think of your life to date in terms of chapters rather than years. What heading would you give to each of those chapters? How much dying was involved in making transitions? How was your life enriched as a result of risking transitions?

3. Has there been a time when you felt that you had come to "the end of the line," but what seemed to be termination resulted in germination—a time of unanticipated fulfillment

and fruitfulness? Why was that experience of "dying" to self a necessary prelude to the opening of a new chapter in your life? What life-changing lessons did you learn?

4. Abiding in Christ entails painful pruning from time to time. What have you found most difficult to give up? Having let go of what you were clinging to, did you find a sense of release?

5. Have you ever belonged to or been aware of a church that has died—and there was no resurrection? Is there any way that its demise could have been prevented? Did it become terminally ill because of denial and refusal to take appropriate steps for its recovery? What could have been done differently?

6. It has been said that a church that lives for itself will eventually die by itself. To what extent is your church preoccupied with its internal concerns? What percentage of its budget is allocated to ministry among existing members and what percentage is spent on local service and outreach as well as global ministries?

4

TEAMBUILDING

WALKING AND WORKING
ALONGSIDE OTHERS

The body is a unit, though it is made up of many parts; and though
all its parts are many, they form one body. So it is with Christ.

1 CORINTHIANS 12:12

Beginning in the 1970s and into the 1980s, I found myself
with management responsibilities in two Christian organizations, but my seminary education had left me unprepared for
the challenges that faced me. In an effort to learn how to lead
people, I avidly read books on leadership and management.
Many contained the acronym PLOC, which stood for Plan,
Lead, Organize and Control. They represented the management style that had built the big, prosperous companies
after World War II. They were geared to the hierarchical, top-
down controlling style that had been the norm for military
strategists as well as for companies involved in the war effort.
This management approach became known as Management
by Objectives.

On the positive side, Management by Objectives strengthened accountability and enhanced individuals' motivation to achieve their potential. The downside, however, was that many lives were destroyed and careers threatened, especially in the more ruthless organizations. Employee loyalty was eroded as more and more demands were made to maximize efficiency and profits. People felt dispensable. Their health broke, their family life suffered, and many ended with burnout, heart attacks and other stress-related problems.

Gradually the realization dawned in the more progressive companies that Management by Objectives had to be seriously reconsidered and reevaluated. It was no longer working, not only because of the human cost involved, but also because it was proving too ponderous a model. It was also de-motivating to many employees. It failed to recognize people as individuals with their distinctive personality, gifting and talents.

Many churches in North America uncritically adopted management models from the business world. This was especially the case among boards of laypeople who transferred their management insights and experience from the corporate world to the church. Pastors were often unduly influenced because their academic training had not included courses on church leadership and management.

The church should function more as a family than as a business enterprise, welcoming people of all ages and backgrounds. It does not hire and fire, and its range of ministries is comprehensive. Leadership in such a context is far more relational and caring of the whole person. This requires building teams.

INTO AND BEYOND THE INFORMATION AGE

The advent of the information age also revealed the old model to be too ponderous and lacking in creativity. Its silo structure prevented creative collaboration, creativity and risk taking. It rewarded success, while failing to recognize the importance of learning through failure. In the old model, failure was likely to lead to rejection and firing. A learning organization benefits more from processing its corporate failures than from celebrating individual achievements.

Some are calling our times the *conceptual* age rather than the information age, because the underlying issue is what to do with all the information cascading upon us. We need skills to sift, discern and establish connections, often across disciplines that previously existed in isolation from each other.

This chapter moves the discussion beyond the information age to address three Cs: conceptualization, creativity and connectivity. The last of these will take us into the next chapter as we broaden our horizons beyond individual churches and faith communities.

PROFOUND CULTURAL UPHEAVAL

Culture itself is undergoing profound changes as we move from automation into the information and imagination age. We now live in an era of instant global communication, with the exchange not just of words but also of images and ideas. A new generation of leaders is emerging as the product of this onslaught, in which knowledge is no longer restricted to a privileged and protective elite who safeguard their information as a means of enhancing their power base and as an instrument of control.

An older generation that operated on the outworn principle of "command and control" has had to learn new, open styles of management that require team building. Those who have been able to change are no longer a controlling hierarchy but serve as catalysts resourcing teams of knowledge workers. They are comfortable working with people who have skills that they themselves don't possess, doing so without feeling personally threatened. The underlying issue goes beyond simple access to knowledge, as we are now increasingly discovering. We become so bombarded with information that we end up overwhelmed to the point of paralysis. The information acquired leads to the need to obtain yet more information to come to a decision. This state of affairs in now known as "analysis paralysis." Reports of information grow in volume until they become unwieldy and need to be summarized. They fall into two main categories: those that gather dust and those that generate momentum. In the church, we can use these categories to see which of our own reports are useful and which are not. "When all is said and done, too much is said and too little is done" applies to so much inaction in our society and our churches.

AN EXAMPLE OF TEAMWORK IN OUR CULTURE

One of my three sons-in-law, Joe, is a paramedic with the Los Angeles Fire Department. From what he has told me about his training and experience, I've learned a great deal about team-building. As a paramedic, he is highly trained in assessing the condition of patients. Sometimes he has to deal with a single victim, while at other times there may be a number of individuals involved in an accident or a major disaster, such as a train wreck. A major accident causing multiple casualties requires setting up a triage center on the site, grading the victims according to the severity of their injuries.

Paramedics generally work as a two-person team, but they are dependent on the contribution of others around them as well. They must be confident leaders, able to accept a high degree of responsibility. To this end, their training is rigorous.

In emergency situations, timing is crucial. They have to be able to assess injuries quickly and take prompt action. In addition, they must know their limitations. They are first responders, not nurses or physicians. Their task is to transfer patients to the ER department of a hospital as quickly and safely as possible, handing them over to qualified medical and surgical personnel for further treatment. To remain at a high state of alertness, they train constantly within the fire station and clean and maintain their equipment for instant response.

We see the same commitment to teamwork in other areas of life, including the sharing of records and consultations between specializations in medicine. The same goes for engineering projects, business plans and investment strategies. But do seminaries and local churches use teamwork as they seek to respond to ministry challenges such as reduced budgets, shrinking pools of volunteers, contentious issues and their increasing marginalization within Western cultures?

How God Operates as a Team

It has become increasingly popular within some Christian denominations to abandon the traditional language of the Trinity as God the Father, God the Son and God the Holy Spirit because of its supposedly patriarchal bias. Admittedly, traditional language can be misinterpreted. But we must be careful not to ignore the biblical use of Father/Son language and not to project our understanding of human sexuality onto God. A very different picture emerges if we redefine our understanding of "Father" and "Son" in relation to biblical revelation.

We recognize that human language, when applied to God, will always have limitations. We have to use a variety of images. However, the alternative proposed in many liturgies—the Creator, Redeemer and Sustainer—is far from satisfactory.

The Persons of the Holy Trinity can't be parceled out into a series of job descriptions. They don't act independently of each other, but in concert and with considerable overlap. God the Father not only planned our salvation but also gave his only Son for the fulfillment of his mission. Jesus repeatedly said that that he was dependent on his heavenly Father and that he followed the leading of the Holy Spirit. The Holy Spirit also reveals the Father to us in intimate terms and is described as the Spirit of Christ. In other words, they act together, not as static entities. They are dancing with rather than marching alongside each other.

Here we find a strong theological challenge to our individualism, which we identified as one of the obstacles in our chapter on hurdling. A hyper-individualistic society may have been appropriate for lone pioneers exploring the West, but it's totally inappropriate in our present cultural setting.

When Renee and I came to Southern California from England in 1984, we were bemused by the widespread preoccupation of the many people around us who were focused almost to the point of obsession with trying to discover who they were. A number sought the help of therapists to lead them through their personal crises of self-identity. We were struck by the loneliness of so many of our neighbors and their suspicion of people who tried to be friendly.

We arrived in our neighborhood thinking that Americans in general, and Californians in particular, were friendly by nature. So we attempted to introduce ourselves as new arrivals to our neighbors, as had been our custom in England. The response to a friendly smile and a personal introduction was usually a person peering at us through a closed screen door. We later read the comment of one Canadian author that "Americans are the loneliest people on earth."

This is not only due to our individualism, but also to the fact that we are such a diverse and mobile society. In fact, we have seen the same disturbing trend developing as we have made repeated visits back to England during the past quarter of a century. One of our African students at Fuller made a perceptive comment when asked about his experience living in the area. He replied, "Americans are very friendly, but they don't make very good friends."

We began to ask ourselves why we had never questioned our self-identity, even when finding ourselves in seemingly dead-end jobs. We came to the conclusion that it was because we grew up in a network of relationships involving our family, neighborhood, church and workplace. That didn't take place in a village or small-town setting, where everyone knows everybody else, but in a city of 350,000 people.

However, the city in which both Renee and I grew up still had a walking culture with local shops, markets, schools, libraries and churches. We often stopped to exchange greetings and chat briefly with people we knew. Where we now live, each of these activities requires getting into a car and rubbing shoulders with people we have never met and will probably never see again. It's quite an event to bump into a familiar person at our nearest supermarket.

Fortunately, a number of city planners across North America are beginning to talk in terms of "new urbanism," which consists of community developments that are multigenerational, are affordable for people at various economic levels and have all essential services available within walking distances. This type of development is not confined to the United States. For example, Melbourne, Australia, is taking the lead in decentralization—this city of 4.5 million is redeveloping into 9 regional centers.

Perhaps the current crisis of global warming will get people out of their cars and into discovering and exploring their neighborhoods. It will take initiatives from below rather than reliance on political pressures, and we can hope that more and more churches will become key players in the action. In such contexts, churches and community-based organizations could play a significant role in fostering authentic community, providing safe and stimulating environments where people could feel that they really belong. This is part of the social dynamic of church growth here in North America. (In my book *ChurchMorph* I detail a number of significant examples of churches capturing the vision and taking up the challenge.)

DISCOVERING OUR TRUE IDENTITY

As people made in the image of God, we will never discover our true identity in isolation. From the very beginning, "God created mankind in his own image, in the image of God he created them; male and female he created them" (Genesis 1:27 NIV 2011). In the account in the following chapter in Genesis, the point is made even more strongly:

> The LORD God said, "It is not good for the man to be alone. I will make a helper suitable for him." . . . But for Adam no suitable helper was found. So the LORD God caused the man to fall into a deep sleep; and while he was sleeping, he took one of the man's ribs and closed up the place with flesh. Then the LORD God made a woman from the rib he had taken out of the man, and he brought her to the man. The man said, "This is now bone of my bones and flesh of my flesh; she shall be called 'woman,' for she was taken out of man." For this reason a man will leave his father and mother and be united to his wife, and they will

become one flesh. The man and his wife were both naked,
and they felt no shame. (Genesis 2:18, 20-25)

This passage emphasizes the complementary nature of male
and female. But this raises the question of singles who feel
called to the single life or have not yet found a life partner.
Should they consider themselves as incomplete, disadvantaged
or even rejected? The feminist movement arose partly because
of the marginalization of singles. As we saw in the opening
chapter, we need to define *family* more extensively, and churches
as "the family of God" have to positively affirm the complementary nature of male and female.

Unfortunately the prevailing leadership model in most
churches is of a "senior" pastor who is usually male. But the
increasing number of females in pastorates does not resolve the
issue. Depending on the gender of the senior pastor, a congregation is liable to present either a masculine or a feminine bias,
resulting in the disenfranchising of representatives of the opposite sex unless they opt for being compliant. In response, I
would argue that there is an urgent need to demonstrate complementary leadership, with both male and female leaders
working in tandem.

Try this out for an entertaining game at a party where people
don't know each another. Pin a number or amusing name on
each person, and ask everyone to walk through the group to
guess who is the spouse of whom, and see how many you guess
right. Often the attraction is not obvious because opposites attract, and I'm not speaking here about dominant partners who
choose a compliant husband or subservient wife. We often
choose partners who make up for our deficiencies.

We have often described our marriage of fifty years as a
yacht. Renee is a quiet and practical person who seldom gets

enthusiastic about anything and is especially cautious about
my poorly conceived and impetuous ideas. She is the keel in the
yacht, providing stability and predictability. On the other hand,
I'm more like the sail, determined to push ahead in response to
every fresh stirring of the wind.

We could easily become frustrated with one another—and
we do—with the keel saying to the sail, "You're just a bag of
wind!" or the sail complaining that the keel is "just a dead
weight." But without the keel, the yacht would be blown over,
and without the sail, it wouldn't move. The existence of both a
keel and a sail is what makes progress possible and ensures the
stability of the vessel. In technical terms this arrangement is
known as an isomorphic fit, the unlikely joining together of opposites. But for the relationship to work, there has to be mutual
respect and appreciation that each has a vital role to play.

TEAMBUILDING

Teambuilding requires great skill and patience. First we have to
recognize the differing personalities of each member of the
team. Some of us are go-ahead extroverts, whereas others are
more reflective, cautious and introverted. Some are task oriented, but with poor relational skills, whereas others are con-
sensus builders.

We also have to recognize that individuals learn in different
ways. The classroom model of learning does not fit everyone.
Intelligence comes in different forms. Some are studious, ana-
lytical and have sharp critical faculties. These individuals
perform well in formal academic programs. My daughter-in-
law has highly developed aesthetic intelligence; she displays
her understanding of color, texture and proportion in her
painting and photography. Others may have great intellectual
abilities but little rational intelligence.

An academic, high-achieving cousin of ours who researches in the medical field failed his driving test on numerous occasions because he has poor spatial intelligence—and he could not qualify as a doctor until he passed his driving test. Fortunately, he eventually managed to overcome his handicap to get his license.

Another of my sons-in-law is by no means an academic, but his relational skills are off the charts. He seems to have an inexhaustible network of people he knows and who enjoy his company. He has the ability to strike up a conversation instantly with a complete stranger. As a FedEx courier, he knows personally many of the individuals on his route. And for a number of years he has worked as a volunteer on the Tournament of Roses Parade here in Pasadena. He mixes with equal comfort with the well-heeled professionals and the ordinary folks, whom he makes feel special.

We have all experienced discomfort when working outside our primary type in areas that require skills and insights that we don't possess. This might be a brilliant academician, strong in logic and conceptual intelligence, who fails to read an audience that processes information in a different way. They may be lateral rather than linear thinkers or may learn best through concrete problem solving rather than through being presented with abstract propositions. There is far more involved than the academician simplifying the technical language he or she might use in the classroom.

I have also witnessed preachers failing to read their audience. Sometimes they are invited to academic gatherings but use the same style of communication they would with their congregation. Their addresses are filled with exhortations, rhetorical questions, exclamation points and homespun stories, but without addressing the critical issues. The same is true for students entering a Doctor of Ministry program after some years in ministry, who struggle to adjust to academic rigor in writing assignments. Their papers read like sermons. We are speaking here of learning to read the audience and how to recognize different learning styles. This is even more complex when addressing other cultures in which different idioms, voice tones, gestures and volumes of delivery prevail. One of my grandchildren struggled through school, but eventually managed to graduate. The classroom environment was an inappropriate place for him to learn. Testing revealed something never evident at school because it was not part of the curriculum: he has a very high technical aptitude. The German and Swiss educational models take this difference into account in their streaming of students, which may explain these nations' technical competencies in industry.

KEY ELEMENTS IN JESUS' TRAINING METHOD

Relationships. With the foregoing in mind, I believe that we have a great deal to learn (read "relearn") from Jesus' approach to teambuilding and leadership development. The first thing we notice on the occasion when Jesus called his first four disciples—all of whom were fishermen, with Matthew the tax collector added soon after—is that his approach was highly relational. His terse invitation was "Follow me!" In modern terminology, he was establishing an apprenticeship model. As the disciples accompanied him, they learned by observation followed by opportunities to ask questions. He was accessible to them, with no prior appointment necessary.

Observation. The disciples saw Jesus perform miracles of healing and deliverance. They listened as he answered questions with questions that often stumped his listeners. By telling his stories and inviting the crowds to listen and think things out for themselves, he allowed them the joy of making their own discoveries, rather than simply providing the answers. What we discover for ourselves with sufficient prompting we are most likely to remember and want to share with others. Experts in a particular field are often too quick with answers designed to reveal their own knowledge or brilliance. Such an approach simply serves to intimidate and silence the group, who think, *Why bother? He wants us to splutter the wrong answer so he can correct us.*

Deployment. The Gospels record Jesus sending out the Twelve ahead of him to prepare for his coming, and Luke added a second mission by a further seventy-two unnamed disciples. Their instructions were very specific, and on their return Jesus conducted a debriefing.

Learning from failures. An apprenticeship can't be completed in one semester of classes. It generally lasts for at least two or three years and is spent learning a set of skills necessary to perform a task with competence and professionalism. This is why our current seminary approach to education needs to be reexamined to translate credentials into actual competencies. The same learning model translates into the life of the church too.

Learning by doing. The most important lessons that the disciples learned were not acquired in the safety of a classroom, but as they encountered different situations and people from many walks of life in the course of each day. Most of these occasions were unscheduled, so they had to learn instant readiness.

Those whose learning is confined to the classroom often want a structured and secure environment for them to feel comfortable and in control in communicating what they know. But learning opportunities seldom present themselves at times that are convenient to us. When the Samaritan woman approached the well where Jesus was sitting, he was exhausted after a long walk, and it was the hottest time of day. He engaged in a lengthy conversation with her despite his hunger, and she returned to her village and reported on the life-changing encounter she had just experienced. The entire population turned out to meet Jesus, with many of them coming to believe in him (see John 4:1-42).

THE APPRENTICESHIP MODEL IN THE EARLY CHURCH

Once apprentices master the basics, they are in a position to become fruitful, in other words to reproduce what they have learned so far from their teachers. That's why Paul on a number of occasions exhorts new believers to become imitators of him (see 1 Corinthians 4:16; 11:1; Philippians 3:17; 4:9; 1 Thessalonians 1:6; 2 Thessalonians 3:7-9).

The relatively new Christians in Thessalonica, who were the imitators of Paul, are themselves imitated, becoming a "model to all the believers in Macedonia and Achaia" (1 Thessalonians 1:7)—that is, their influence spread throughout the area we now know as Greece. The church spreads with the speed of an influenza virus. It's evident that the message was being heard loud and clear over a wide area as it rang out from them with the urgency and clarity of a trumpet blast.

The Christians of Thessalonica were not only clear in their message; they were also credible in terms of their kingdom values: "your work produced by faith, your labor prompted by love, and your endurance inspired by hope in our Lord Jesus Christ" (1 Thessalonians 1:3). In the next chapter we'll see how the early church was structured to facilitate this momentum.

As Timothy took responsibility for leadership among the churches of Asia Minor, Paul spelled out that he expected the process to continue from one generation of believers to the next, saying, "The things you have heard me say in the presence of many witnesses entrust to reliable people who will also be qualified to teach others" (2 Timothy 2:2 NIV 2011). Paul worked with a team whenever possible. It's instructive to go through the book of Acts and his letters and collect the names of individuals who were his coworkers. They included seasoned leaders as well as the young Timothy. When new faith communities were formed, these churches already had a model of shared leadership to emulate. And no doubt Paul included them as local expressions of the model he had introduced to them by entrusting the care of congregations to them. This presents a challenge to many of our churches today that have demonstrated the single or senior pastor model and then attempted to transfer to a shared model of leadership.

LESSONS FROM THE COMMISSIONING OF THE FIRST DISCIPLES

When we look at the disciples whom Jesus commissioned to continue his mission in his meeting with them in Galilee, some important lessons emerge that apply to teambuilding and team functioning in any age and context (see Matthew 28:16-20).

Failure need not be final. The first disciples were a restored community that had come through hard times in which they had deserted and denied their teacher. This reminds us that failure need not be final. In fact, God's "power is made perfect in weakness" (2 Corinthians 12:9). When we are at our weakest, we are in a humble learning mode.

We are worshipers first and workers second. The disciples were worshipers. Within an academic environment, both lecturers and students need to recognize that their work is always an outcome of their worship. This marks them off from the secular rationalistic academic environment. It also carries over into the church in relation to the conduct of business on the boards and in the vestries of our churches. Worship is an essential part of the work, not simply a perfunctory prelude to the agenda.

Teams are inclusive and welcoming. It's unlikely that Jesus and the disciples were alone on this commissioning occasion. There may have even been a large crowd. Paul refers to large numbers of "the brothers" at one occasion after Jesus' resurrection and before his ascension into heaven, which surely also included "the sisters" and children: "After that, he appeared to more than five hundred of the brothers and sisters at the same time, most of whom are still living though some have fallen asleep [died]" (1 Corinthians 15:6 NIV 2011). The larger crowd surrounding the inner core kept the core group accountable, but it also was the unnamed wider circle of disciples, whom I believe are eventually included in his Great Commission.

Teaching is inclusive. It's neither selective nor merely theoretical. Jesus' teaching is meant to be obeyed, not merely analyzed. The early Jewish Christians had blocks of teaching gathered by Matthew in his Gospel that enabled them to work through the implications of following him within their Jewish cultural context. The early churches springing up throughout the Mediterranean world had to work out the implications for themselves, which is why Paul's letters are both doctrinal and practical in content. We have to undertake the same disciplined approach to understanding the implications of following Christ within a twenty-first-century, pluralistic context as non-Jewish followers of Jesus did.

The apprentices are not abandoned. Jesus promised to go with the disciples and to continue with them at all times and in every situation. His ascension into heaven was followed by the gift of the Hoy Spirit at Pentecost. He comes to each believer irrespective of age, gender or race. Are church leaders prepared to trust God to fulfill his promise to be with them today?

CHARACTERISTICS OF A HEALTHY TEAM

Members of healthy teams are committed to one another on a personal level and to the common vision that has brought them together. This creates strong bonds of mutual accountability. Their vision is both clear and contagious. Others become inspired and want to get on board.

Each team creates its own chemistry—that is, its own ethos arising out of the challenges of its task and the contribution of each of the team members. The members don't vie against each other to gain attention or outperform each other. Such a competitive attitude within a team serves only to undermine trust. Once that is allowed to happen, the team quickly falls apart or succumbs to a dominant personality. Healthy teams empower each of the members as well as inspire those with whom they come in contact.

Leadership is about influence, and influence comes about through making connections and forging links. Building sustainable and productive teams requires the contribution of a visionary, a facilitator, an enabler and an appraiser. Together they create a synergy that is unique to that team.

Many books that address teambuilding focus on building a professionally trained leadership team, which is the practice in most large churches. However, many seminary-trained pastors were educated on a competitive and individualistic model. Here our concern is with teambuilding *throughout* the congregation. It entails transforming a predominant consumer mentality to one in which the congregation becomes "a team of teams." This is in keeping with the concept of every-member ministry that is so strongly emphasized in the New Testament. Many church leaders and members believe in the *concept* of every-member ministry, but their churches are not structured to enable it to emerge.

A number of impressive examples have come to my attention in recent years of churches decentralizing their ministries and encouraging the formation of mission teams engaged in a wide variety of projects. In *ChurchMorph*, I described the cluster concept that originated at St. Thomas Crookes and the Philadelphia Centre in Sheffield, England. That same idea has been adapted by a number of other churches, both in England and in North America.

A well-functioning family operates as a team, with each member—no matter how young—playing his or her part. The family provides a context in which to grow as a person in the midst of accountable relationships. Ideally, it's a supportive community that provides encouragement, issues challenges, offers advice, requires accountability and makes corrections. The church as the family of God needs to find ways to ensure that these same elements are in place. This task becomes even more challenging when the prevailing family environment fails to offer these elements. The church then has to teach and demonstrate family-life skills.

QUESTIONS FOR THOUGHT AND DISCUSSION

1. The reaction against the "command and control" style of management has led to confusion about the very idea of leadership. Consequently, potential young leaders are backing away because they don't want to emulate the older style of leadership, and many organizations are experiencing severe difficulties in identifying the next generation of leaders. What can we learn from leadership within the early church that can provide healthier models for the renewal of the church and wider society?

2. What challenges does the advent of the information age pose

for leaders who learned teambuilding skills in different times? How can we avoid being overwhelmed by information to the extent that it paralyzes rather than stimulates action?

3. How can the contemporary church benefit from team leadership as exemplified in the early church? What are some of the threats to team leadership's effectiveness? How might these threats be anticipated and avoided?

4. How does the concept of teamwork relate to the trinitarian nature of God? In what ways has undervaluing and even ignoring the significance of community for human well-being had a detrimental effect on society? What role might the church play at the local level in restoring community? In what ways is the church placed so it can play a key role?

5. What can we learn from Jesus' example in training his disciples as a team and his commissioning of them to make disciples in the entire world? How did this apprenticeship model prepare them for later leadership among local churches? How can you apply the key elements in his training model to your own church?

5

NETWORKING

Expanding Our Horizons
in a Shrinking World

All the churches of Christ send greetings.

ROMANS 16:16

We live in a networked world. I see this as our children—
and to an even greater degree, our grandchildren—are on
Facebook, YouTube and Twitter, communicating with friends
near and far. They are amused that we, their parents and grandparents, don't seem to be interested in social media. But pastors
in youth and family ministries use these interactive media to
keep in regular contact with the young people in their groups
as well as to engage in conversations with casual contacts.

Every day—and in this I'm not exaggerating—I receive invitations to be someone's online "friend." I confess that I have not
responded to any of them, even though some invitations are
from people I know well and whose contributions I value. The
fact is that I'm not a computer addict, and I just don't have the
time. I have to be face-to-face for fulfilling conversation. I guess

I rely quite a bit on body language and voice inflection. Or, more likely, I grew up in the pre-computer age, so I'm intimidated by social media. I use the computer primarily as a word processor, which has saved me from filling wastepaper baskets with countless typed revisions.

THE EARLY CHURCH AS A NETWORK

A question has been bugging me for the past few years: why did the dynamic and rapidly growing early church gradually degenerate into a static, institutional church? Although it continues to expand at the edges, it seems to have lost much of its momentum in its older, more established parts.

Within the New Testament, we see the main centers of influence shifting, first from Jerusalem to Syrian Antioch and then from Ephesus and Corinth to Rome. In North Africa, Alexandria became a center of Christian thinking and mission outreach. (Unlike Islam, Christianity has never had one permanent home base.)

With the spread of Christendom, the church was absorbed into the political order, and its message became compromised as its structures became increasingly institutionalized. Throughout the Western world, we now find ourselves increasingly in a post-Christendom and neopagan, religiously pluralistic culture, in which the old Christendom model of church is struggling to survive.

The network structure of the early church was able to flourish because of the vastly improved communications under Roman rule—namely, the construction of a road that connected all parts of the Roman Empire and increased safety in travel through the strategic stationing of Roman troops and the imposition of Roman law. The growth of the church was exponential in that every local church had the capacity to reproduce and the connectivity to provide mutual encouragement. Despite hostility and occasional outright persecution, the church was able to continue to expand.

SPIDERWEB NETWORKS

We must not imagine the early church's network structure as a fishing net. Rather, its organizational network consisted of dispersed "nodes" linked by threads. In other words, they resemble an intermingling of spiderwebs. Some of these nodes were more widely connected and influential than others. However, there was no central node that controlled or organized the rest. The nodes were dispersed and related to each other in a dynamic way. Their intrinsic authority lay in their power to influence and not control. Richard Mouw, president of Fuller, describes this influence as "convening power."

As with modern blogging sites, some webs are far more influential than others. Some flourish for a time and then drop in popularity or are discontinued, while at the same time others are emerging. A network is dynamic and fluctuating, not static and predictable.

Brian Jackson of the RAND Corporation has studied the varied organizational structures of networks in terrorist organizations. He identifies the following forms, which I will relate to the organizational structure of networked churches both in the early centuries and in the contemporary church.

Chain link. Some church networks are chain link, with one group influencing the next. The challenge here is to convey the DNA of the original group along the chain without it becoming weakened or divergent. The further along the chain, the more difficult it becomes to ensure orthodoxy and accountability.

The early church faced this challenge with the rapid expansion of its networks, with some groups embracing unorthodox beliefs and with disagreements causing division and infighting. This led to the appointment of bishops, elected initially within individual churches, who then began to exercise wider authority. They were both mission leaders and troubleshooters. As household churches replicated within a city, the bishop took on responsibility as overseer of all of them. Later his ministry extended still further, as he traveled to meet with other bishops to address common issues. My son-in-law Brian Auten is an intelligence analyst with expertise in the operation of insurgents, and he makes the important observation that the bishop (or overseer) didn't, however, centralize the meeting place. There was no organizational control center. And within a hierarchical structure, the further from the center each link was, the more difficult it became to control or to provide accountability.

Hub and spokes. A second organization pattern evident in many denominations and megachurches is that of the hub and spokes network, in which a number of churches (spokes) relate to a central church or leader (hub), which gives them a sense of belonging and identity. A number of previously independent congregations might elect to become part of this kind of network. Some are more motivated by what they can benefit from in such an arrangement than by what they can contribute to strengthen and enrich both the hub and the spokes. Consequently, they drain energy from the movement and cause it to stall rather than add impetus. Increased mass does not always translate into increased momentum, but may simply be a dead weight.

The early church seems to have been loosely organized on a hub and spoke system. At least there were recognized centers of influence, but not of control. We find hub churches in Syrian Antioch, Corinth and Ephesus. The church in Thessalonica evidently had widespread influence, even though it was only months old at the time when Paul wrote his first letter. From them "the Lord's message rang out from you not only in Macedonia and Achaia—your faith in God has become known everywhere. Therefore we do not need to say anything about it, for they themselves report what kind of reception you gave us" (1 Thessalonians 1:8-9).

The church in Ephesus, where Paul spent two years, became the center of a cluster of churches in Asia Minor. While there he "had discussions daily in the lecture hall of Tyrannus . . . so that all the Jews and Greeks who lived in the province of Asia heard the word of the Lord" (Acts 19:9-10).

The key element in this dynamic is the example set by Paul and his companions in constantly moving the churches forward, not only by exhortation, but also by example. In the following chapter we will return to the strategic significance of apostolic leadership for the church today—and the crippling consequences of its neglect.

All-channel. A third organizational pattern is the *all-channel* network, in which every group is linked to every other, without a single center. The group with the greatest influence at any one time depends on the contribution it's able to provide for the benefit of all. Or it's the group that has initiated a gathering of the network to share insights or address common problems.

The relative strength of the coupling between individual congregations and between different networks also varies. Sometimes the coupling is strong to the point of holding each other accountable to common goals and shared values. At other times it is much weaker and may be temporary.

Dwight J. Friesen has come to the counterintuitive conclusion that a number of weak links are more sustainable and less vulnerable than one strong link. He invites us to consider an island linked to the mainland by one single, multilane bridge. Should that bridge become damaged or encounter a traffic jam, the island becomes isolated. However, if it's linked by a series of smaller bridges, there are alternative crossing points.

THE HOUSEHOLD STRUCTURE OF EARLY CHURCHES

The typical structure of early churches was based on the household. Churches were often identified by the name of the head of the house in which they met. When we modern readers see the word *household*, we think of a domestic family unit. But within the world of the New Testament and until the Industrial Revolution, the majority of business and manufacturing took place within the household or workshop. In other words, households were the basic building blocks for the economic well-being of a community.

Who, then, were the people who made up a typical household? First was the *extended family*, with three generations represented (if they had survived). Also the household would consist of uncles, aunts and cousins, as is the case throughout much of the Middle East, Africa, Latin America and Asia today.

In addition were the *indentured laborers* or *slaves*. We have to think in first-century terms and not base our assumptions about this group on what we know of the slaves transported from Africa to North America. It's estimated that 80 percent of laborers in the Roman world were indentured. This helps us better understand the discussions of slaves in the Pauline letters.

The way in which slaves were treated would of course depend on the character of the head of the household and his sphere of influence. No doubt, some slaves were treated harshly and abused. But many were treated with respect, to the point that some slaves in the church in Thessalonica, for example, were apparently taking undue advantage (1 Thessalonians 5:14;

2 Thessalonians 3:6-7, 11). For many slaves, the household provided identity, security and dignity as well as opportunities for social mobility, especially when the household had a good reputation. Consequently, many freed slaves opted to continue in service within the family. The household also included hired help and occasional laborers who hung about, hoping for temporary employment, errands to run and goods to transport. In the early church, rich and poor, male and female were regarded as brothers and sisters in Christ. They exchanged the "kiss of peace" irrespective of social divisions. In writing to the Thessalonians, Paul urged all the believers to "make it your ambition to lead a quiet life, to mind your own business and to work with your hands, just as we told you, so that your daily life may win the respect of outsiders and so that you will not be dependent on anybody" (1 Thessalonians 4:11-12).

In his second letter to them, Paul was even more forthright in his warnings against idleness, his own life providing an example.

In the name of the Lord Jesus Christ, we command you, brothers and sisters, to keep away from every believer who is idle and disruptive and does not live according to the teaching you received from us. For you yourselves know how you ought to follow our example. We were not idle when we were with you, nor did we eat anyone's food without paying for it. . . . For even when we were with you, we gave you this rule: "The one who is unwilling to work shall not eat." (2 Thessalonians 3:6-8, 10 NIV 2011)

There was a great deal of trading between families, either through monetary payments or exchange of goods, which brought Christian and non-Christian households together. Commercial and social interactions were not sharply separated in the ancient world, because there was a strong element of relationship building to establish trust, as well as culturally expected social politeness. To get immediately down to business would be considered rude; this prevails today in many cultures. In this way non-Christian households could observe the impact of the gospel. This helps us understand Paul's insistence on Christians living their corporate life in a Christlike way. This leads us to a fourth circle, which we might call *friends of the family*. The large urban centers of the Roman world included cities with populations of a quarter of a million or more that were crowded, rowdy, dirty and at times violent. They had their own version of neighborhood watch: vigilantes who were often retired soldiers. People knew their neighbors because they lived in such close proximity, shopped in the street-level market stalls, took care of their laundry in the same place and ate at the corner eatery, where they drank wine and shared local gossip. McDonald's was not the first fast-food enterprise.

Many poorer families lived in one-room apartments where cooking facilities were rudimentary and the lighting of fires was dangerous. In fact, fires were frequent and disease was rampant; earthquakes were catastrophic. The uncertainties of life helped build a sense of community.

NETWORKS HELP FACILITATE EXPONENTIAL GROWTH

The household structures of the early church contributed significantly to its growth. In his extensive study chronicled in the book *House Church and Mission: The Importance of Household Structures in Early Christianity*, Roger Gehring noted that each household church was limited in size by the seating capacity of the location where it met. In a typical Roman villa with an atrium, a capacity crowd would number about thirty-five with the lounges against the wall to maximize space. Churches meeting in storefronts may have had room for only fifteen to twenty people, if the fourteen storefronts excavated in Corinth are typical.

Consequently, if the Christian movement were to spread throughout a city, it would have to be by establishing a network of household churches. Such networks were supported by the fivefold ministry that is described in Ephesians 4:1-16. There was no equivalent in the early church to the megachurch phenomenon that has gained such prominence across North America and elsewhere in the world.

Each household church was led by the head of the family, who would have received instruction from Paul or one of his disciples. Many of them were further guided in their leadership by the type of correspondence preserved for us in the New Testament, where we find twenty-one examples of letters dealing with a wide range of doctrinal and practical matters.

The leaders of this network of churches not only led worship but also organized common meals, local charity work and disaster relief, especially during epidemics, when pagan families often abandoned their sick relatives.

Paul and others also made return visits to congregations to provide further guidance and encouragement. The stated purpose of what we have come to know as Paul's second missionary journey was to go to Lystra, Iconium and Antioch in Pisidia (today's southeastern Turkey), "strengthening the disciples and encouraging them to remain true to the faith" (Acts 14:22). Paul's third journey was also undertaken initially with the purpose of strengthening the churches in Syria and Cilicia (see 15:41), but he then continued through Turkey to Greece.

Roger Gehring identified the following house churches and their leaders as recorded in the New Testament: Philippi: Lydia and the jailer; Thessalonica: Jason; Corinth: Aquila, Priscilla, Titius Justus, Crispus; Cenchrea: Phoebe; Ephesus: Aquila and

Priscilla; Rome: Aquila and Priscilla (again!), Aristobulus, Narcissus; Colossae: Philemon; and Laodicea: Nympha.

MISSION AND THE HOUSEHOLD CHURCH

The growing network of household churches throughout the major urban centers meant that the church was in public view within each local community. Neighbors could observe churches in action, see their mutual support and be recipients of their hospitality and generosity. The household churches were also accessible, in that they were close by and people would feel at home in them, because the places of meeting were just like their own households.

These churches allowed for rapid expansion because church growth didn't depend on financial resources to buy or lease real estate. They met wherever space was available and accessible. And the style and location of meeting were appropriate to the social context.

A question then arises: Is the household concept for the expansion of the church relevant in the twenty-first century? In our diverse and pluralist urban environments, the church needs to express social diversity. One size does not fit all. The household also challenges the dualistic mindset that separates the sacred and the secular—one of the prevailing heresies of modernity.

The church also needs to multiply points of contact by taking the initiative in becoming involved in all aspects of community life and being seen making a transformative impact. We also need churches small enough for everybody to feel that they are valued, that their questions are welcomed and that they can make a contribution to expand and deepen the various expressions of ministry.

The serious challenge we face today in older, traditional denominations and in many independent churches is that our model of church is not easily reproducible. It's too expensive, consumerist and controlled. It also is increasingly out of step with a networking, relational culture.

There is a growing realization within some traditional denominations that the time has come to give permission for nontraditional expressions of church. Experimental forms of church need to relate to the wider culture, raise local leadership and reproduce from day one. This phenomenon is increasingly evident among newer networks that are springing up. And these two streams are drawing inspiration increasingly from each other.

SCATTERED BY PERSECUTION

The growth of the church throughout its first two hundred years is an impressive story. The book of Acts provides us with an anticipation of what Jesus expected to happen: "But you will receive power when the Holy Spirit comes on you; and you will be my witnesses in Jerusalem, and in all Judea and Samaria, and to the ends of the earth" (Acts 1:8).

When we turn the pages of Acts to trace the unfolding of this outline, we discover that the growth of the church didn't result from strategic planning. There was extension into Samaria, but the significant growth came as a consequence of persecution, which appears initially to have specifically targeted the Greek-speaking congregations in and around Jerusalem. This occurred after the martyrdom of Stephen as an effort to arrest the further spread of the movement. But it had the opposite effect: "Those who had been scattered" by the persecution in connection with Stephen traveled as far as Phoenicia, Cyprus and Antioch (Acts 8:4).

The other striking characteristic of the expansion of the early church is the initiative of the Holy Spirit in propelling the church forward. At every significant stage, the church moved forward, sometimes reluctantly, hesitantly and spontaneously as various groups were taken by surprise by the Holy Spirit's unanticipated leading in new directions. But the church was responsive because it was prayerful, obedient and bold. (For some striking examples, see Acts 2:1-12; 10:1-48; 11:1-18; 13:1-3; 16:6-10.)

When we look at Bible maps of Paul's missionary journeys, we might get the impression that it was all preplanned. But while he did target key centers of population and influence, it seems that he "followed his nose" and retraced his steps in accordance with need. He was not constantly on the move, but rather stayed in some places for months. In other words, he didn't have a preconceived, tight schedule, but was flexible and responsive to the leading of the Holy Spirit. For instance, it was in response to a visionary call that Paul crossed from Troas into Europe (see Acts 16:6-10).

Hierarchical organizations create top-down dependency structures that are vulnerable to persecution. Take out the top leaders, and the rest collapses like a pack of cards. Or when major disagreements arise, the structure becomes fragmented or polarized into warring factions. In contrast, network organizations present a much greater challenge to those who seek to penetrate and destroy the movement. Today we see this as security forces attempt to deal with terrorist networks.

It was the network structure of the early church that made it so resilient as well as reproducible. It was fed and supported by a number of centers of influence or "nodes," as we have seen in our overview of the book of Acts and the Epistles. Its ability to reproduce at an exponential rate resembles that of the starfish.

Ori Brafman and Rod Beckstrom draw the distinction between the spider and the starfish. Because a starfish has no central nervous system, you can cut off its tentacles and each will grow into a complete starfish. The fourth-century North African church leader Tertullian observed something similar happening in the early church: "The blood of the martyrs is the seed of the church." In other words, the more you attack the church, the more it grows.

Each early household church also was in constant communication with a broader network of households and individuals. They didn't exist as exclusive entities, sealed off from wider society.

THE LIMITS TO BOUNDARIES AND CONTROL

In their business literature, Margaret J. Wheatley and Myron Kellner-Rogers have written of the importance of maintaining porous boundaries. They argue that boundaries should not be regarded as barriers of protection, but rather as places of meeting and exchange.

We can all think of the disastrous consequence of controlling parents who attempted to determine their offspring's careers and had a predetermined profile of who they would or would not marry. As parents and grandparents, Renee and I have come to recognize that even at the extended family level, it's counterproductive to attempt to control the lives of our offspring. They need the freedom to make their own decisions and to live with the consequences. When our children were younger, we established values and laid down boundaries, but as they grew, they needed to decide on their own careers and life partners. They may not be the individuals we would have chosen, but then we have to pause and remember that our parents didn't think we made the right choices either.

In fact, my mother worked for Renee's father in the carpet-laying trade. They didn't get along, to the point that my mother left for other employment. When we began to be attracted to each other, we had no idea that our parents even knew each other or that Renee's dad was my mom's manager. Happily, when we became engaged, they were reconciled.

RESOURCING NETWORKS

For networks to grow and new ones to form, they need to be resourced in a variety of ways. This is accomplished through a number of channels. The most widespread and influential of all is the shared Internet sites that are visited by hundreds and even thousands of younger leaders who work within new and expanding networks. The individuals and groups who manage these sites are sometimes professors in seminaries, but more often they are visionary leaders who share their own latest thinking as well as provide links to other key resources.

Another important contribution is made by short-term, mid-weekly gatherings (sometimes called boot camps) of leaders involved in establishing new ministries or gaining a vision to begin one. These events are not designed for theoreticians but for practitioners.

I had the privilege of meeting with a group of about two hundred church planters, representing one of these networks called Ecclesia. Its origins were at Virginia Tech, where the large, campus-based church has encouraged new graduates to find jobs and work together to birth new faith communities around the country. The energy level of those young church planters was incredibly high, and their questions and comments were very perceptive because they arose out of their experiences. I held a voluntary additional gathering for any who wanted to hear about my experiences of lessons learned from fifty years of ministry. Due to the crowd, extra chairs had to be brought into the room—an indication of widespread hunger for relational mentoring. In West Hollywood and Santa Monica, there are already three new congregations established by this network.

A further significant development with great potential for creating a new generation of missional leaders is the emergence of nonaccredited schools and seminaries offering certificate courses. These function in low-income areas and are designed to serve storefront churches and urban ministry organizations such as Global Impact. These schools make high-quality ministry training and theological training both available and affordable.

Their concern is not to train leaders for future ministry but to mentor them in their current ministry. Such schools emphasize spiritual development and mutual prayer support. The students recognize their need for a network of fellow students who struggle with the same issues as they do within the challenging context of urban deprivation, violence and the need for a transformative gospel that relates to the whole of life.

Harvest Bible University is near Skid Row in downtown Los Angeles and is hosted by an Evangelical Lutheran church. Its ministry is to urban church leaders and those called to leadership in local churches and urban ministry development. I learned about the school from my oldest son, Steve, who registered as a student in their associate's degree program. The faculty consists of volunteers—over half of whom are Fuller graduates—and also teachers from the graduate student body and professors of neighboring accredited schools.

Harvest Bible University was approached about receiving accreditation through the sponsorship of another university, but decided not to accept the offer, because it would impose too many restrictions that would remove it from the very people it was trying to help. Tuition is kept to an absolute minimum, with a two-unit course costing seventy-five dollars. Beginning with programs at the associate level, students can progress to a master or a doctor of ministry degree.

I had the privilege of teaching one of the evening classes and was deeply impressed by the energy level of the students and their commitment to one another. The courses are demanding, especially for students who have struggled through formal schooling. All the sessions are videoed, and copies of the DVDs go to sixteen correctional facilities, where vetted students who have committed their lives to Christ are preparing themselves for ministry both among fellow inmates and on their release to the outside world.

We have attended two of the graduation ceremonies in support of Steve, which were full of celebration, gave glory to God and provided testimonies of those whose lives had been profoundly impacted by their studies, including former inmates who had studied with Harvest Bible University while in prison.

The challenge of identifying and training the next generation of leaders is not confined to inner-city and immigrant churches, but has become an increasingly urgent challenge within older, traditional denominations. Their seminaries are doing a competent job in providing leadership for established congregations. But the majority of the traditional churches the pastors are serving are aging and declining, with an increasing percentage of those small churches unable to pay a living wage and to service the debt accrued during the long years of the pastor's expensive education.

Alternative programs need to be in place to train leaders of local churches through intensive evening and Saturday courses, so they can function with biblical knowledge, theological insight, and an appreciation of the history and the riches of their own tradition, as well as be able to address ethical challenges presented by our relativist society. But of equal importance, we need leaders who are able to reimagine the church in the increasingly post-Christendom cultural settings in which they will have to operate with far leaner material resources and without the benefit of a full-time salary.

For the past five years, I've played a small part in one such pilot project in the presbytery of Santa Barbara, called the Lay Leader Training Institute. A West Coast Presbyterian seminary has sponsored this certificate program. The typical student is a session member, some are on the presbytery, and a few are engaged in new church development as commissioned lay pastors. Once again the energy level is incredibly high, with perceptive questions and in-depth discussions.

Each class has about a dozen students, which is appropriate at this pilot stage. But other presbyteries, who want to learn from this program, already are showing interest. Sessions are now being videoed at high quality to make the courses available by extension, and plans are afoot for live podcasting. This innovative program currently receives accreditation through Fuller.

For most of this chapter, we have examined the growth dynamic of networked churches within the context of the New Testament. Imagine the increased potency of networks that are linked by instant Internet communication. This is the dynamic we see increasingly at work in our own day, linking churches across traditions and around the world. Online classes are growing in popularity because they make ongoing education both affordable and accessible. The quality of online courses varies enormously. Some consist simply of text delivered in the lecture room and then transposed to an online format.

Making courses available online requires the redesigning of the material to make it more interactive. Students need to be organized into cohorts with chatrooms in which they can exchange ideas and critique each other's work. Professors need access to the ongoing discussions. Students are required to post work a certain number of times each week. They also need to receive grades regularly to assess their progress. Finally, whenever possible they need opportunity to meet in one- or two-week intensives, face-to-face with the people in their chatroom and the entire class. Such well-run classes attract high-quality students who are being equipped for ministry while also undertaking ministry.

Such innovative approaches potentially provide valuable resources to local churches wherever they are, enabling them to be faith communities in the process of lifelong learning in which knowledge can be related to wisdom and the issues of the day.

QUESTIONS FOR THOUGHT AND DISCUSSION

1. What networks of churches do you see operating within your own tradition? To what extent do these networks extend beyond your denominational boundaries?

2. Are you a part of, or aware of, different types of networks as described by Brian Jackson—that is, chain link, hub and spoke, and all-channel? What have you perceived their strengths and weaknesses to be?

3. What are some contemporary equivalents of the New Testament household churches? What are some of their strengths and potential weaknesses?

4. In what ways did the household structure of the early church facilitate its rapid expansion? Are there lessons from their example that can be transferred to the contemporary challenge of reproducing faith communities to reach large seg-

ments of the community that the institutional church is failing to reach?

5. To what extent is Western culture becoming less friendly toward the Christian church, or at least refusing to give up its privileged position in a pluralist society? How is the church responding to this change in attitude?

6. In what ways is the church being provided with educational and training resources to face the new missional challenges? What additional resources would you like to see made available?

6

COMMUNICATING

CREATIVE ENGAGEMENT IN
EVERY AREA OF LIFE

Therefore, if anyone is in Christ, he is a new creation;
the old has gone, the new has come!

2 CORINTHIANS 5:17

Despite all of the impressive church buildings and congregations throughout the country, despite access to the mass media through radio and television, and despite the fact that a significant percentage of the population is in church on an average Sunday—with still more claiming allegiance to the Christian message—we still haven't done a very good job of communicating the essence of the gospel and conveying its transforming power into our society.

Evidently there are some serious blockages. For the most part, we are restricted to talking to ourselves, or at least we fail to make sense to the wider community that has little or no contact with the institutional church. Our life-transforming message seems trapped in the church "bubble" as we become increasingly culturally irrelevant.

GETTING TO KNOW THE CULTURE AND THE ARTS

As Renee and I think back to our childhood and adolescent years, it became apparent that we grew up in a culturally limited environment. Even more than a decade after World War II, heavy restrictions applied in every area of life until the mid-1950s. Our schools had no local sports facility, no theater with a stage—just an assembly hall with a podium, which doubled as the gymnasium. There was no school orchestra or band. Art consisted of one forty-five-minute period during which we were encouraged to paint.

My family never went to a musical concert or live theater performance, with the exception of the Christmas Pantomime, consisting of slapstick comedy loosely based on nursery rhymes; that great British tradition still survives to this day. I never learned to play an instrument, but Renee had some piano lessons as a child. She was a little more fortunate in that she had an older sister who took her occasionally to the theater and the ballet. Neither of us was introduced to serious literature.

My one diversion as a child was the Saturday-morning matinee at the local movie theater, costing ninepence (about ten cents), where we watched Roy Rogers and Gene Autry cowboy movies, Laurel and Hardy and the Three Stooges comedy capers, and Flash Gordon in his space adventures, as he was propelled in a rocket shaped like a large World War II bomb and apparently powered by sparklers. But it all looked so realistic to us kids. It was always a letdown when we emerged into the cold light of day to resume our small-world, humdrum lives.

But we did learn to use our imagination as we lost ourselves in comics and adventure tales and sat around on an evening "watching" the wireless (that is, the radio; and yes, we actually sat and looked intently at it). We impatiently listened to the hum of the valves as the set gradually warmed up, anxious that we not miss anything. Sixty years later we have more vivid memories of the children's programs and serial mysteries than we do of much more recent and elaborate TV dramas.

My one entry into the higher realms of culture was when I joined the choir as a treble in our local Anglican church through the influence of a school friend. This lasted until my voice began to break—and it has never fully mended, as my wife and children can attest.

Yes, we were certainly deprived culturally by today's standards. But what you never had, you didn't miss.

We now look at our grown children and eight grandchildren, wondering where all their creativity came from. How different is their world today. Our children were delayed in discovering their creative talents, mostly because of our own cultural limitations as parents. However, we were fortunate in that two of our daughters were friendly with a classmate who lived just a few doors away. Her mother was a cellist with the London Philharmonic Orchestra and encouraged them with their music on the flute and violin. She also took them to orchestra rehearsals.

Our son, Steve, became friends with a classmate who dreamed of a career in movies; they shot home movies together. His friend then became an assistant director at Pinewood Studios. From those early days, he has continued in the movie industry, becoming the executive producer of the latest James Bond franchise.

Steve has never lost his enthusiasm for filming and today makes high-quality videos of his vacations and provides the church website with video clips. His wife is a very talented photographer and watercolorist. And all our children have gradually blossomed in musical talent, both singing and playing a variety of instruments, in artwork, in clay modeling, in writing stories and poems, and in expressing themselves with artistic sensitivity in interior home design.

We have also been amazed to see our grandchildren flourish from a young age, writing lyrics and composing songs, singing in school and church choirs, playing a variety of instruments, performing on stage. Our granddaughter Ashley was in a joint-schools production of an original Broadway production of *All Shook Up!* that combined Elvis Presley songs with a Shakespearean drama. We contrast their resources with those we so sadly lacked in our day—their marching bands, orchestras and theaters in which to stage dramas and musicals.

Renee and I can't help but contrast our experience of appearing before an audience with that of our grandchildren. In contrast to their poise, confidence and creativity, we were terrified to be on stage. We still have a black-and-white photograph from our teenage years when we were assigned to sing a duet in costume at a missionary meeting. The duet turned out to be a solo because I could not produce a single sound, I was so nervous.

Or I think of an even more embarrassing occasion when I appeared on stage in a religious drama to confront another of the performers on the state of his soul. Unfortunately, I walked right past the individual I was supposed to address according to the script. Realizing my mistake, I turned around and promptly forgot my lines. Within ten seconds, I had turned a drama into a farce. The audience could not recover their composure, so it was "curtains." Fortunately, they were a friendly crowd of young people who enjoyed the hilarity.

Such experiences stemmed from the fact that self-expression, public performance and confidence in the presence of adults were not encouraged. Most of us were lacking in self-confidence, well beyond today's young people. Creativity and imagination need to be nurtured from a young age, before little ones become inhibited by self-consciousness. Yet it needs to be restrained at times so that it does not degenerate into precociousness.

CREATIVE THINKING AND FORMAL EDUCATION

Parents and teachers of small children are aware of the high levels of creativity demonstrated by the young ones in their care. With appropriate stimulus and encouragement, their creativity can begin to blossom at an early age. However, if the children's initial efforts meet with complaints about "messiness" from adults or their expressive art is ridiculed or ignored, their creative potential may not only frustrated, but severely damaged or destroyed. They feel rejected and that their best efforts are never good enough to please their parents or teachers. In fact, Renee's school motto was, unbelievably, "My best is not good enough for me!"

We would expect that the more education a person benefits from, the more creative they will become. Unfortunately, the evidence points in the opposite direction as far as formal schooling is concerned. Sir Kenneth Robinson is a world-renowned researcher who has studied the negative impact of education on creativity. From high levels of creativity, students drop off to extremely low levels of creativity by the end of graduate education. They may have gathered more knowledge and skill but little in the way of wisdom and creative insight into what they are going to do with what they have so painstakingly learned.

The overwhelming emphasis throughout our educational philosophy in the Western world is on the development of left-brain activity to the neglect of the right brain. We are trained to think logically in a linear fashion and required to memorize more and more information, much of which does not appear to have immediate or long-term relevance to life. Higher education becomes narrowly focused as we withdraw into our specializations, so that we end up learning more and more about less and less. During times of economic recession with reduced budgets for education, the first part of the curriculum to face severe cutbacks is often in the arts. A rationalistic and materialistic society regards such programs as peripheral. This is a serious error, as we know, for instance, that there is a close link between musical and mathematical abilities. It is a shortsighted policy, according to many educational experts, because the arts are the very programs that stimulate the imagination and creativity that will be vital for developing research and innovation in the twenty-first century.

Robinson argues persuasively that this conceptual age requires fresh skills, so students need to emerge from our schools and colleges able to use their imaginations, think creatively and establish links between seemingly unrelated disciplines. This is where so many groundbreaking discoveries are and will be made in the coming decades. Also educators need to recognize that intelligence comes in different forms, not just logical, but also spatial, social, artistic and so on. And each requires a distinct approach to learning.

A CHANGE IN MY WAY OF TEACHING

This realization has had a profound, if belated, impact on my own approach to teaching. In a ten-week quarter system, there is insufficient time for students to prepare adequately for class. However, within the doctor of ministry program, a radically different approach becomes possible, because students are required to do extensive reading before attending the related intensive class.

This is what I've been attempting to do during the past couple of years. The preliminary but vitally important step is to encourage students to take responsibility for their own information gathering and sifting before they attend the one- or two-week intensive class. Class time is not primarily devoted to the dispensing of information; it's a waste of both their time and mine to plow through information that is readily available. In other words, we have to move from pedagogy to an adult learning model.

What then do we do in the classroom?

1. We review the topic for the day, highlighting the main points.

2. We invite clarification questions.

3. We identify the points that are most significant for our various ministry situations. This is best done by means of small discussion groups. Then each group records on the whiteboard the issues they want to consider further.

4. We step back and exercise discernment in terms of the relative importance of each and then ask what is missing from the list that we might want to add.

5. We integrate these insights with our wider reading, including books and articles from other disciplines. In other words, we are learning to think laterally, not just linearly. The current student generation is more skilled and less inhibited in these exercises than previous generations.

6. We work as teams to see if we have come up with any new insights as we have thought "outside the box."

If the class has worked for the students, they emerge with fresh passion. This is the acid test for whether they are passionate: are they simply wearied by their education and focused on their grade point average, or have they matured and become more integrated in their understanding of themselves and their calling to ministry?

This approach is not confined to academic contexts but relates directly to the integration of faith and life within the context of the church, as we will see.

MADE IN THE IMAGE OF THE CREATOR GOD

A number of years ago, I was challenged by a single sentence in a book on communication: "We go to the Bible for our *message* but not for our *method*." That simple statement got me thinking, so I decided to read right through the Bible asking just one question: "How does God communicate with us?" I discovered that God is a multimedia communicator, which eventually led me to write a book summarizing my findings, called *The God Who Communicates*.

It's surely significant that God made this statement: "'Let us make mankind, in our image, in our likeness, so that they may rule over the fish in the sea and the birds in the sky, over the livestock and all the creatures that move along the ground.' So God created mankind in his own image, in the image of God he created them; male and female he created them" (Genesis 1:26-27 NIV 2011). These verses come at the climax of the creation story. Three times the statement is made that we are made in God's image in order to ensure that we get the message.

We could dwell on different ways to understand what is signified by "the image of God," but the context emphasizes the fact that there is a divinely planted creative potential in each and every one of us. This creativity needs to be recognized, celebrated and developed within the community of faith. Unfortunately, it's all too frequently ignored, denied or threatened by insecure leaders.

RELEASING THE CHURCH'S POTENTIAL TO COMMUNICATE

In chapter two, on hurdling, we looked at Ephesians 4:1-16 from the standpoint of the obstacles that the church encounters as it attempts to become an authentic missional community in Western contexts. In this chapter we will focus on the central part of that passage, verses 11 to 14, from the particular standpoint of the church's ability to communicate within the wider world.

Questions are often raised as to how the fivefold ministry matrix in Ephesians applies to ministry today. Do apostles and prophets occupy a prominent place, or did their significance dwindle with the death of the Twelve and the writing and distribution of copies of the letters and Gospels that became the New Testament?

My personal conviction is that twenty-first-century ministry should not simply be a carbon copy of ministry in and through the first-generation churches of the New Testament era. I believe that the five spheres of ministry identified—apostle, prophet, evangelist, pastor and teacher—continue to play a vital and foundational role, and the ways in which they are expressed catalyze fresh expressions in our changing culture.

We will look at each sphere in turn from the perspective of creativity in worship, mentoring and witness. Worship acknowledges the source and inspiration of our creativity. It also ensures that "performers" don't become intoxicated by their "audiences," but rather seek to divert attention away from themselves to the God to whom they are answerable as stewards of the gifts entrusted to them.

Also, I'm focusing on the five spheres, not as separate offices in the church, but as essential functions that are part of a full-orbed ministry in which all participate through the local church. On the practical level, this means that individuals who function in each area may not claim the title and would be uncomfortable being so described. Whereas Protestant churches have emphasized "the priesthood of all believers," the Roman Catholic Church since the mid-1960s has increasingly emphasized the importance of "the apostolate of the laity."

Let us now look briefly at the apostle, the prophet and the evangelist in relation to the church's communication with the surrounding world.

THE APOSTLE AS GROUNDBREAKER

Apostles not only make a personal impact, but also invest in the lives of others, generating faith communities within their spheres of influence.

First, let's look at the apostle who is called to the entertainment world. In the absence of the media apostle, the church is left largely singing to itself and playing to the home crowd. I write these words just a couple of days after a U2 concert at the Pasadena Rose Bowl. Is it a stretch of the imagination to consider Bono to be a functional apostle, getting the message out beyond the sanctuary into the stadiums, music stores and iPhones of the world? For the concert, 100,000 people crowded the stadium, but even more impressively, more than 14 million watched the show live on electronic devices.

The artistic media apostle inspires others. Individuals and groups of all levels of ability take up the songs, and some move beyond mere imitation to explore their own insights and develop their own distinctive sound.

Celebration has played an important role in worship throughout the ages. The term "new song" has great significance (see Psalm 40:3; 96:1; 149:1; Isaiah 42:10; Revelation 5:9). New songs are in response to the gracious initiatives of God in the manifestations of his saving power and awesome majesty.

They are traditional or modern hymns, songs infused with fresh potency, or spontaneous compositions under the direct inspiration of the Holy Spirit. Verse three of Psalm 33 proves that skill and exuberance are not mutually exclusive: "Sing to him a new song; play skillfully, and shout for joy." God's response to King David's cry for mercy strengthened him to declare a new song: "My heart leaps for joy and I will give thanks to him in song" (Psalm 28:7).

New songs provide an intensity of celebration that can't be confined within the gathered community, but spills out far and wide. Indeed the nations will be invited to participate and even gather spontaneously; new songs reach out to the nations and through future generations (Psalm 96:1-3, 7-10; 97:1; 100:1; Isaiah 2:1-3; Micah 4). A number of the psalms call on the whole creation to join in the jubilation. In heaven the new song has already begun and will continue throughout eternity, sung by all those who have been "redeemed from the earth" (see Revelation 5:9; 14:3-4).

The apostle is called to places where the church has no voice or influence. Some apostles operate within the business and manufacturing world. They create new companies or influence existing ones as salt and light, seeking to change a corporate culture to reflect kingdom values of personal integrity, respect for the individual, and corporate honesty and trust. Apostles are culture creators rather than simply culture critics, which is a transition that the church needs to make, according to Andy Crouch, the author of *Culture Making*. This is what the Roman Catholic Church envisions in expanding the "apostolate of the laity."

Such apostles would benefit from theological training to help them develop a full understanding of the good news of the kingdom inaugurated by Jesus. They need to recognize that God always precedes us and that we therefore need discernment to recognize where God is already at work, often through the most unlikely individuals and groups. This understanding of apostolic ministry extends into every area of life. Might this suggest a need for new curricula offerings in seminaries? The approach would need to be flexible to be accessible to people with jobs—from shift workers to corporate executives. The presence of such people in our seminary classrooms would raise new questions and force our academic institutions to relate more closely to the pressing issues of the day.

THE PROPHET AS POET AND LYRICIST

Prophets are most frequently identified as proclaimers and preachers. Their style is typically regarded as confrontational. They declare their message with divine authority, often prefacing their pronouncement with statements like "Thus says the Lord."

However, when we turn to the prophetic books of the Hebrew Scriptures, we find that the typical style of the prophetic word was not that of a narrative sermon. It has taken me a long time to notice the obvious, possibly because my generation was reared on the King James Version, in which the messages of the prophets appear in prose form.

When we turn to the *Tanakh* (Jewish English Translation), the New Revised Standard Version, the New International Version or the New Living Translation, or any other form of Scripture, we find that the bulk of the prophets' words are not composed as prose but as poetry. This holds both for the Major and the Minor Prophets.

Unfortunately, much poetic structure, beauty and literary impact is lost in translation. The various meters in the Hebrew express different moods, provide plays on words and display vivid imagery that don't readily carry over into another language and culture.

Poetry can often penetrate our human defenses more than prose due to its economy of words, its novel turn of phrase and its evocative imagery that stirs our feelings and prods our imagination. Good poetry is never predictable. A poem sticks in the memory and becomes a companion, speaking anew as our life situations change. Its impact may be heightened and its appeal broadened when the poet works with a musician, so that the music gives wings to the words. Poems are savored, not simply analyzed.

The preacher must not be allowed to become the sole interpreter of a poem. Turning poetry into prose destroys the power of the medium. It's like explaining a joke. Poetry needs to be restored to the prophet.

The Evangelist as Storyteller and Ballad Singer

We live in a generation that's no longer familiar with the Grand Narrative of Scripture or with the content and significance of Jesus' message and ministry. Consequently, evangelists in Western contexts have to operate much like those working in areas where the gospel has not yet penetrated. They have to become the storytellers. Drawing from the Scriptures, they have a plentiful supply of stories; the Bible has far more story lines and images than the *Lord of the Rings* trilogy or the internationally acclaimed *Downton Abbey* TV series.

Unfortunately, most formal academic preparation tends to deaden imagination. Our seminaries need to rediscover the power of the story and train students in the art of storytelling alongside exegesis and exposition.

On one occasion, I was leading a seminar at a seminary in Johnson City, Tennessee. It was my first visit to Appalachia, and I was in town the same weekend as the National Storytellers Convention. Johnson City has a town-hall-style building de-

voted to storytelling year-round, and once each year they hold
the convention, which attracts thousands of people.

My hosts kindly bought me a ticket to the convention, which
gave me the opportunity to spend two-and-a-half hours listening
to storytellers. Each person had fifteen minutes to tell his or her
story. I was so enthralled that it was hard to drag myself away.
There was rapt attention from the capacity crowds, including
people of all ages. The stories were full of human interest, flashes
of humor, dramatic enactment and deep insights into human
nature. And there I was, an Englishman, with no appreciation of
Appalachian culture, entering into their life experiences.

In the same way, storytelling evangelists can speak to the
hearts of those outside Christian culture. I have a friend in
Glasgow who came to recognize that God had given him an
extraordinary gift for telling stories. It took him some time to
overcome his understanding of ministry as preaching. He now
gains the attention of large crowds in movie theaters and even
soccer grounds with his stories, which are really parables. After
you have stopped laughing, you start thinking.

I must confess that I'm no fan of country western music, but
I can't deny its popular appeal. The tunes are uncomplicated
but catchy. It's the story that grips you, despite the fact that so
many are really depressing. On a long car ride, I sometimes
listen to Johnny Cash's *American IV: The Man Comes Around*.
Many of the lyrics are as memorable as they are disturbing. The
very beat hammers the message home.

Much of our contemporary worship music is celebrative in
nature, and that is appropriate. But it needs to be balanced by
ballads that tell the Bible stories in memorable form and that
allure listeners outside the church. Just think of the abiding
and widespread appeal of Andrew Lloyd Webber and Tim Rice's
Jesus Christ Superstar and *Joseph and the Amazing Technicolor*

Dreamcoat. Musicals have a wider appeal than stage plays. The music, lyrics and dance routines combine to create a lasting impression. And the songs live on in the minds of the audience.

On a recent visit to Vancouver, I met Jason Hildebrand, a Canadian actor who performs stunning one-man performances depicting biblical events and parables. I warmly commend his short film *The Prodigal Trilogy*, in which he casts the story in a contemporary format, playing the role first of the younger son, then of the elder son and then of the loving father. Each scene lasts just seven-and-a-half minutes and is riveting.

In reviewing the gifts of apostle, prophet and evangelist, I've emphasized their significance beyond the local worshiping community as channels of communication into the many worlds that make up a cosmopolitan society. However, the use of these gifts doesn't arise independently from the church, but through the ongoing teaching and pastoral ministries within each faith community. It's there that ministries are birthed, nurtured and held accountable.

Christian character needs time to develop and mature for the gifts to be expressed appropriately. There will be missteps along the way, and early attempts may not be that impressive. Each person requires training, mentoring and honest evaluation. I wonder how many people who began to explore whether or not they had a gift were ridiculed and became disheartened.

These ministries usually are active on the local level only. Where there is recognition of the vital importance of each sphere of ministry and a creative environment is sustained, with individuals supported in the discovery and development of their gifts, ministries emerge that gradually gain widespread recognition. It's difficult to predict what ministry will become popular among the unchurched. God has a habit of raising up the most unlikely individuals.

THE TEACHER AS INTEGRATOR, COMMENTATOR AND EMPOWERER

The pulpit no longer provides the platform from which the neighboring community and beyond can be addressed. Its message seldom reaches beyond the dwindling ranks of the faithful, and sometimes it even falls on deaf ears in the pews.

Within a traditional seminary curriculum, the main emphasis is on fulfilling academic requirements. At one level I have no problem with this goal, because the present and future demands of ministry will require a broader and deeper knowledge base to meet the intellectual challenges, moral dilemmas and missional opportunities of the twenty-first century.

However, as mentioned earlier, we need to ensure that our training is balanced, recognizing the development of both left-brain and right-brain functions. With the overwhelming emphasis in our classrooms still on the imparting of information, students transfer the same teaching approach into the churches they serve. Most of our teaching is modeled on the way we ourselves were taught.

Also we have to face the persistent challenge that academic credentials don't always translate into ministry competence. This criticism is not confined to theological training, but has also been strongly voiced in relation to MBA programs as well as medical and nursing programs. Yet in many ways business and medical schools are ahead of most seminaries in integrating theory and praxis.

This issue became evident in the course of equipping over one hundred trainers as part of the two-year Mission England project that ran from 1982 to 1984. This was an ambitious undertaking seeking to mobilize churches across England in local church evangelistic initiatives in preparation for six Billy Graham Missions held in the spring and summer of 1984. (The usual term "crusade" was inappropriate in the UK context.) Two one-day courses were developed that would be taught across the country. One was provocatively titled "Is My Church Worth Joining?" (The US version of this course used in the late 1980s and 1990s in preparation for a number of Mr. Graham's crusades was revised to "Building a Church Worth Joining." Our North American advisers felt that it needed a more positive ring.) The second course was entitled "Caring for New Christians." Each of the six regions hosting Graham in a soccer stadium selected a team of trainers who were then gathered for a national three-day seminar to train the trainers, who would in turn care for the many inquirers who would respond to Graham's evangelistic invitations.

As we evaluated the performance of the individuals selected as trainers, we were surprised to discover that the most effective were not the well-known preachers and teachers, but those working in parachurch agencies such as InterVarsity, the Navigators, Youth for Christ and Scripture Union, who actually had training skills.

I place myself in the preacher/teacher category, and I had been one of those responsible for the development of the courses with my work in Bible Society. I learned a lot about training from this second group (i.e., the parachurch trainers) during those months.

In the classical preacher/teacher model, the focus is on the expertise of the individual, which means the communication must be informative and even entertaining, but it's seldom empowering. In fact, it can simply breed a following.

I wonder what would happen if our leaders were to receive

further instruction as trainers who could identify the gifts and calling of members of their congregations and provide mentoring opportunities and apprentice them in teams that provide guidance as role models. That could be profoundly empowering. It would reveal who were the potential apostles, prophets and evangelists as well as teachers and pastors within their congregations.

Some churches have grasped these insights, and it's those places that consistently provide a stream of leaders in the various fields of ministry. No doubt you can identify examples within your own church network. This is increasingly clear among the new networks of churches that are springing up across North America, Europe and Australasia.

The voices of the apostles, prophets and evangelists—groundbreakers, poets, lyricists, storytellers and ballad singers—create the "buzz" within the broader culture and at a popular level that provides the teacher with the opportunity to explain, integrate and apply the message. Teachers operate at various levels, but primarily they examine texts at close quarters, line upon line. They then stand back to place stories, poems and letters within the context of the Grand Narrative of Scripture.

Teachers within the local church don't simply dispense knowledge, but also apply their messages with wisdom and discernment, and then call for an appropriate response. In regard to the gifts already discussed, they provide a theological, biblically grounded explanation of each, emphasizing their significance throughout the centuries and also providing cautions regarding misunderstanding and malpractice.

Within the church context, we teachers who were seminary trained need to learn to transition from pedagogy to adult learning models. This is more on a "need to know" basis, addressing the question "How do the biblical narrative and the theological issues raised impact my daily life?" As with most other disciplines, we need to keep pace with the advance of knowledge and develop new skills. A four-year academic program can't provide an adequate knowledge base for the next forty years. We need not just a four-year program, but also a forty-year program—in other words, a serious commitment to lifelong learning.

Denominations, presbyteries and local churches need to network at the local level to make such training available and to evaluate their effectiveness in cooperation with seminaries. This is their investment in the future and can bring rich dividends. It's beginning to happen, and seminaries need to invest heavily to provide from their rich resources. Otherwise they will end up training many unsuitable people in inappropriate ways.

THE PASTOR AS DIAGNOSTICIAN AND CARETAKER

The role of pastors is closely linked with that of teachers. Teaching is never simply academic, but relates to the needs of individuals and communities. It always carries a personal and practical application.

The five spheres of ministry—apostle, prophet, evangelist, pastor and teacher—don't exist as separate entities, but with considerable overlap. For example, the apostle may speak as the prophet and fulfill the role of evangelist. In confronting David, Nathan told a story to penetrate the king's defenses and to address the delicate personal issue of his adultery with Bathsheba. As a prophet, he confronted and rebuked the king, while avoiding a frontal attack. Having told his story, he became the pastor in challenging David personally, saying, "You are the man!" (2 Samuel 12:7).

Pastors deal with individuals one-on-one, eyeball-to-eyeball. They bring heaven in contact with the heart. Unfortunately, and sometimes with disastrous consequences, many high-profile public ministers have not had the benefit of pastoral guidance and become vulnerable due to their independent spirit and increasing celebrity isolation.

The church urgently needs to rethink its understanding of ministry and mission. The good news inaugurated by Christ is too important and radical a message for us to keep to ourselves. We need a fresh outpouring of the Holy Spirit as well as training and skill development for the church to proclaim its message boldly and in the context of the culture—wherever people gather and wherever communication networks are located. We need to communicate on all five channels and to follow God's multimedia strategy of communication.

QUESTIONS FOR THOUGHT AND DISCUSSION

1. Think over the past month and assess how much you have spoken about your faith to other Christians compared to communicating with friends and people who have yet to hear or respond to the good news of Jesus Christ. In what ways can you become a better bearer of good news?

2. Why does the church find it so difficult to communicate its message effectively beyond its four walls?

3. What imaginative and creative examples have you seen or been involved in that communicate the good news in a variety of ways? What media did they employ, and how effective were they in attracting people's interest and making them think?

4. Look up Sir Ken Robinson's website at <http://sirkenrobinson
.com/skr/> or go to <www.ted.com/talks/ken_robinson_says
_schools_kill_creativity.html>. Have your creativity and
imagination been stimulated as a result of the education you
have received? In what ways?

5. Can you think of examples of apostolic groundbreakers in
the entertainment or business world that are translating the
kingdom message and values into their contexts? What are
their methods, and why do you think they are effective?

6. Within a highly secular and at times cynical culture, what
contribution can the prophet as poet and the evangelist as
storyteller make to penetrate people's defenses?

7. Why is the contribution of pastors and teachers so crucial to
the communication process?

7

RECOLLECTING

STAYING OPEN TO
GOD'S UNEXPECTED PLANS

But be sure to fear the LORD and serve him faithfully with all your heart;
consider what great things he has done for you.

1 SAMUEL 12:24

From time to time along life's journey, it's good to retrace our steps. We don't do this to live in the past, but to learn from it. Some people look back with remorse or even bitterness, thinking of their wrong decisions and missed opportunities. But we mustn't dwell on the past, and God will continue to meet us in our current circumstances. The only place to start again is where you are now.

Many of us can look back in gratitude for the grace God has bestowed on us over the years. *Grace* in its biblical sense has fallen out of use in popular speech, so we need to remind ourselves of both its prominence and its significance throughout the Bible. In fact, grace is a dominant theme from Genesis to Revelation, though it is almost exclusively a New Testament

word. This short word is rich in meaning, speaking of the un-
deserved, overwhelming generosity and patience of God.
In popular usage, its meaning has been weakened. You may
be given grace to turn in an assignment later than the due date.
A gracious person is one who is considered polite and consid-
erate. The biblical definition of the word is much stronger. It's
God's acceptance of a person unconditionally. Grace was extended to the human race at an inconceivably high price, for
God so loved the world that he gave his only son (John 3:16).
We most frequently think of grace in regard to our initial
salvation experience. The key text that comes to mind is from
Paul's letter to the Ephesians: "For it is by grace you have been
saved, through faith—and this not from yourselves, it is the gift
of God—not by works, so that no one can boast" (Ephesians
2:8-9). Yet the Bible constantly reminds us that God's dealings
with us both individually and as a community of faith are
always on the basis of his grace and not of our deserving (consider John 1:17; Romans 5:17, 20; 6:14; Philippians 1:7; 2 Timothy
2:1; Hebrews 4:16; 2 Peter 3:18).

GOD'S WAY OF GETTING US WHERE HE WANTS US

Throughout the Bible we see numerous examples of God
working in unlikely places through the most insignificant of
individuals. He seems to choose people who are easily overlooked. In looking for a future king for Israel, Samuel first had
to eliminate the most obvious of Jesse's seven elder sons and
then send into the fields for the youngest to be brought before
him (see 1 Samuel 16:1-13). This principle also holds true in
God's choice of Israel as his special people to convey his message
to the world. Israel was an insignificant, even despised, people.
    Then consider the first disciples Jesus selected. None of them
had formal religious training. They were not from Jerusalem

but from the northern province of Galilee. Among them were four fishermen and a tax collector. Who could have guessed what they would become in the course of following Jesus and being empowered by his Spirit? Here is one of the joys of teaching children and encouraging young Christians: we have no idea how God may be at work in their lives or in his purposes for them.

As with the disciples, so in the case of the first churches to spring up around the Mediterranean world. Paul described the believers in Corinth in the following terms:

> Brothers and sisters, think of what you were when you were called. Not many of you were wise by human standards; not many were influential; not many were of noble birth. But God chose the foolish things of the world to shame the wise; God chose the weak things of the world to shame the strong. God chose the lowly things of this world and the despised things—and the things that are not—to nullify the things that are, so that no one may boast before him. It is because of him that you are in Christ Jesus, who has become for us wisdom from God— that is, our righteousness, holiness and redemption. Therefore, as it is written: "Let him who boasts boast in the Lord." (1 Corinthians 1:26-31 NIV 2011)

The rest of this final chapter tells my story and reveals some things I've learned along the way, particularly about how God works in truly mysterious ways. Of course, your story will be very different from mine, but I hope you will take this opportunity to do some reminiscing of your own and that you will see the unfolding of God's plan in new ways.

I was at the US Air Force recruiting office in Redlands, California, in support of my then nineteen-year-old grandson, who was making his application to join as an airman. He was handling the interview well with a competent and friendly recruiting officer, and while he was filling in answers to form after form, suddenly my mind flipped back fifty-three years, to the time when I was in a similar situation, but in very different circumstances.

Unlike my grandson, I wasn't being recruited; I was being drafted. The place was England, and the year was 1956, when Britain was still recovering from World War II and we were facing the threat of the new Cold War with Russia. At that time every young man of eighteen was scheduled for two years of compulsory military service.

MY EARLY YEARS

I was an inner-city kid living in Nottingham. Although my parents didn't attend church, they sent me to Sunday school. There was a high moral standard in our home. I never heard bad language, and they enforced a strict moral code. At Sunday school the girls sat on one side of the hall and the boys on the other. The only contact between the sexes was by flicking paper pellets when we thought the teachers weren't looking.

Our Sunday school superintendent conducted the worship and prayers from the platform, sometimes to the amusement of his students. First, he had a habit of saying his Hs in the wrong place. So each week we prayed for sick children who were absent because they were "hill." Second, he had ill-fitting false teeth, which rattled when he sang. On more than once occasion he lost them entirely and had to scoop them up in his handkerchief, much to our delight. But we didn't poke fun at him, because of his great love for us kids. When Renee and I were in our late teens, he beamed with delight as he saw us walking hand-in-hand.

My dad was a car mechanic, and when I was sixteen he told me it was time I earned my living in the world. Very few of us had the opportunity of further formal education in those days. As I approached my sixteenth birthday, the school principal asked me what I wanted to be. I replied, "A policeman, sir." He responded, "You don't want to be a policeman. Get a job at Boots Pharmaceuticals." And that is all the career guidance I received. I worked in a laboratory for that chemical and pharmaceutical company for two years before I received my military call-up papers.

When my grandson's recruiting officer asked him why he wanted to join the US Air Force, I thought it was a no-brainer. The Royal Air Force pilots were my boyhood heroes. I knew that we owed our lives and freedom to the bravery of the Spitfire and Hurricane fighters who had saved Britain from invasion and defeat. From the age of eight, I must have drawn hundreds of pictures of RAF planes shooting down German fighters and bombers. But I remember always drawing lots of parachutes, with the Germans landing safely. I didn't want anyone to get hurt or killed. My childhood world was not violent.

I was born eighteen months before the beginning of World War II, and my father, who was in the British version of the National Guard, immediately had to report for duty and served for the next six years in the Royal Electrical and Mechanical Engineers (REME), maintaining military vehicles on bases around Britain.

During the evacuation of the British Expeditionary Forces from the beaches of Dunkirk, my dad was stationed at Dover

Castle. Weapons were in such short supply that Dad's unit was issued with dummy wooden rifles. They asked what they were supposed to do with them if and when the Germans landed. They were told, "Hit them over the head." I don't know whether that story was true, but that was my dad's version.

Among my earliest memories was the sound of air-raid sirens wailing at night. They warned us that German bombers would soon be overhead and gave my mom time to get me out of bed and carry me across the road to some convenient caves in the side of a sandstone rock face. The pub was built into this rock, providing cool storage for their beer. (Today, if you go to the Broadmarsh shopping mall in Nottingham, you can visit these caves and see the living conditions.)

We had frequent air raids. They didn't primarily target Nottingham, but the cities of Derby eighteen miles away, where the Rolls Royce aircraft and tank engines were made, and Coventry, which was so essential for the war effort. Most of the bombs dropped on Nottingham were either off target or simply off-loaded so that they didn't have to be taken back to Germany.

Thinking back sixty-five years, I can still remember the first time I spoke to an American. During the war and for a decade afterward, we faced severe rationing of food, clothes and—to the keen disappointment of us kids—candy. The big deal was to approach an American serviceman and ask, "Got any gum, chum?" I must have been around five or six before I plucked up enough courage. With my mom watching me from a distance I nervously asked for gum, which I had never tasted. But I thought it must be good, because every American I saw seemed to be chewing constantly.

To my delight, he gave me a single stick of Wrigley's chewing gum. Now I was faced with a dilemma: should I chew it or save it? I was unlikely to get another stick of gum in the foreseeable future. I decided to chew it, but saved the wrapper as a souvenir. At the end of the day I was still chewing on it, so my mom put it on a spoon for the next day. Eventually, it became a health hazard, so my mom got rid of it. Strangely, I've never liked gum since.

By this time in my grandson's interview, he was being asked about his education as I had once been asked about mine. I struggled throughout school in the lowest-ability stream and then was promoted to the next stream up from the lowest level in my grammar school, which I entered by just scraping through the first big exam we had to take at age eleven. We didn't have graduation ceremonies and transcripts. At sixteen we took General Certificate of Education exams in each of our subjects, set not by the high school but by the University of Cambridge examiners. I managed to pass in six subjects, but my grades were all Cs and Bs. By English standards, that wasn't bad, because you had to be an absolute genius to get an A; I don't remember anyone who achieved that standard. I could identify with my grandson who had faced similar challenges in his formal education.

LEARNING DISCIPLINE

The RAF officer processing me saw that I wore glasses, which meant many jobs were not open to me, so he said I'd have to become a typist for the next two years. The immediate challenge was that I had never typed a word in my life. At school, all our work had to be in pen and ink, in our best handwriting.

The ten weeks of basic training was a challenge for most recruits, but especially for me. I was an only child, with my dad away in the war for six years. My mom was a cleaning and tidiness fanatic. She cleaned every room in our four-room row house every morning before she went to work sewing and mending carpets in a furniture store or in stately homes. She did everything for me: washed and ironed my clothes, cleaned my room, and put everything away in my drawers and wardrobe. I wasn't allowed to disturb a thing. Now here I was in a Quonset hut, issued with my full kit to maintain and display for inspection, each item folded in a perfect square.

My two RAF uniforms were not of the quality of US Air Force dress uniforms today. Those of us serving just two years were issued rough serge material, rumored to be left over from World War I. Ironing and keeping knife-sharp creases in that material required some skill and great patience.

Our boots were not the lightweight fatigue boots of today, but pimply, heavy leather clodhoppers. I swear the manufacturers made sure the leather was especially rough to make us work harder on them. By first drill parade, we had to work so hard on those boots that the drill sergeant could see his face in the shiny toecap. How did we bring about the transformation? By melting polish over a candle, and spitting and polishing for hours on end. Then we set out on a march over rough ground, getting them all scraped up, so that we had to do the same thing again to be ready for the next morning's parade.

Every week our billet was inspected. In preparation we polished the floor with thick wax polish, after which we skated around on felt pads so that we didn't make any marks. We cleaned all the windows with newspapers, and removed every speck of dust. We soon learned that the first thing the inspecting officer did as we stood to attention by our beds with all our kit displayed was run his finger along the top of the door. If there was dust there, you got yelled at and had to start again. He was the only cleanliness fanatic to outdo my mom.

I grew up in a gun-free society, even as an inner-city kid. The first real gun I ever saw was the rifle issued to me in basic training. It was a heavy old thing. When you fired it, the kickback was like that of a mule. If you didn't hold it properly, it was likely to break your collarbone.

I have other basic-training stories of physical exercise early in the morning in the freezing cold, parade-ground drills, long marches, being dumped in the mountains of North Wales with just a ground sheet (a useless L-shaped piece of oilskin that soldiers in the World War I trenches had to keep them dry) and instructions to find our way out to a predetermined point in twenty-four hours. I still have a photo of that occasion.

USEFUL SKILLS FOR LATER IN LIFE

As I've walk through life, I've often found myself having to do and learn things that at the time don't seem to have much relevance. I did them because they were forced on me. But as I look back, I am grateful that I gained that knowledge and experience. At the time I had no idea just how useful they would prove to be one day.

After ten weeks we were deemed fit to be seen in public and went home for a week's leave before beginning trade training. Remember, I had been assigned to train as a typist and clerical worker, and those first weeks were boring, boring, boring. We were set behind old clunky typewriters with a mask over the keyboard, and we began typing ASDFG to music with a slow beat. When we mastered that, we moved to the right hand, typing HJKL. So we learned to touch type the entire keyboard without being able to see the keys. The instructor walked up and down to see how many mistakes we were making and listening for any keystroke that was out of time with the music. As we progressed, the instructor increased the tempo of the music until we could type at the required speed and accuracy to pass the typing test.

We then advanced to learning the page layouts of all the letters and memo forms that had to be precisely spaced. Every letter to an officer ended with

> I have the honor to be,
> Sir,
> Your Obedient Servant.

I think the course lasted for fifteen weeks, and I was so relieved to get it over with. Yet those basic skills have served me well over the years. Later, as a full-time student and then as a professor who has written fifteen books, I didn't have access to a computer until I was forty-seven. But I sure could type.

LEARNING TO KEEP CONFIDENCES AND DO A GOOD JOB

After basic training, I received my assignment. I was posted to an RAF establishment that evaluated new aircraft and weapons systems that the RAF was considering purchasing from manufacturers. As a nineteen-year-old, I was sent to a group of eight specialists who worked as a team to evaluate new aircraft in the course of production. There wasn't much in the way of electronics in those days: one officer dealt with engines, another airframes, another armaments and so on. The two officers above me were a fatherly warrant officer and a Squadron Leader in charge of the unit.

My job was simply to type rough draft after rough draft and then produce the final version of the report to send to the Air Ministry. Much of the work was highly classified, so I had to learn responsibility and confidentiality. But the information was safe with me because I didn't understand a word of the technical jargon. On the wall of our unit was a World War II cartoon poster to remind us of the importance of keeping our lips sealed. It showed two airmen drinking at the bar, chatting together. The head of one was a donkey. The caption underneath said, "Remember, the jawbone of an ass can slay a thousand men." That's from the Bible, by the way (see Judges 15:15).

In two years I prepared reports on the RAF's first jet trainer, the American Sikorsky helicopter built under license in Britain; the P-1 English Electric interceptor with a top speed of over 1,300 miles per hour; the Saunders Row SR-2, which proved too expensive; and last of all the Folland Gnat. I didn't see any of those planes until about four years ago, when my daughter and son-in-law took me to an air exhibition in San Bernardino, California, to see military aircraft from around the world. And there to my amazement was the Folland Gnat, a tiny interceptor.

My years as an RAF typist taught me the need for care and accuracy. Every spelling mistake had to be hand corrected on three carbon copies. The final version was typed on onionskins, during which you removed the typewriter ribbon, allowing the keys to cut the letters. Any errors had to be corrected with a fluid we called boob juice. (The word *boob* meant "mistake" in those days.) The skins were then rolled over an ink-covered drum from which you made your copies. It was a laborious process, and the copies had to be both clean and accurate. How I love the convenience of my computer and printer today!

PREPARED FOR ANY EMERGENCY

In addition to the daily duties, we had to serve either on armory guard or fire watch duty on a weekend once a month. This meant lying on your bed for most of the time, reading or doing "Egyptian P.E."—that was disrespectful RAF slang for horizontal ceiling inspection, because absolutely nothing happened. Usually.

On one occasion the son of my Group Captain (colonel in US ranking) ran into the house in the officers' married quarters to announce to his mother that there was a man in the sky coming down with a parachute. She tried to shoo him away, believing it was simply make-believe. But with his insistence, she went outside to see the airman descend. I was one of a detail sent out that night—which was cold and rainy, of course—to guard the wreckage of the aircraft until it had been inspected and carted away.

For fire drill we had all been taught the rudiments of fire-fighting, never expecting we would have to use them. But on one dark and stormy night, we had a fierce thunderstorm, and the sirens over our fire station began to wail. We all clambered into our oilskins and donned our fire helmets, and with bells clanging we roared into the officers' married quarters. A house had been struck by lightning, and the roof was already ablaze. The parents were out for the evening, leaving their two teenage daughters asleep in bed. They appeared at the window, ready to leap to safety. It was quickly decided they could be caught only by a commissioned officer.

Once they were safely out of the house, we began to attack the fire with our fire hoses. Fortunately, we had a couple of trained firefighters to direct operations. The front door was axed open, and I was told to run the fire hose up the stairs. On the way up, I skidded on the wet stairs and tumbled to the bottom step. When I reached the top, there stood my Squadron Leader tweaking his very RAF moustache, smartly dressed in his blue blazer. He looked at me and remarked with a twinkle in his eye that I will never forget, "Ah! Gibbs, I see that you are a man of many parts!" For the next week, back at the office, he found it difficult to hide a smile as I made him his morning cup of tea.

STARTING AT THE BOTTOM

Some people are fortunate enough to be born into a privileged life. They have the social or educational advantage to skip ground-level jobs. But there are valuable lessons to be learned by starting at the bottom of the ladder, which an increasing number of leadership training models promote.

During my second year of service, I applied to go on a weeklong leadership course run by the RAF Chaplain's School. Permission was granted, and that provided a further learning experience.

My time in military service was just a brief two years, but they were life changing in many ways and set the direction for the rest of my life. I realized that afresh as the recruiting sergeant talked with my grandson about his potential opportunities. I began as aircraftman second class—the very bottom of the food chain—was promoted to first class, then to leading aircraftman and finally to senior aircraftman.

I had entered the RAF with a growing conviction that my vocation would be that of a pastor in the Church of England. The church authorities had checked me out before I left for military service, and during my trade training I was allowed to visit a theological college for two days. I learned that I had to continue with my education before I would be considered.

While I was in the projects team, I eventually shared my sense of vocation with my Squadron Leader. He replied, "As you know we have times when we are all under a great deal of pressure to produce our reports. But then there are some weeks when we are all away and you are here alone. Once all your work is complete, you can fit in some of your studies." Most evenings I went to the education building and studied alone by correspondence courses through Wolsey Hall, Oxford, and the London Bible College to get my Advanced Level General Certificates of Education so that I could go on to seminary and eventually earn a bachelor of divinity degree as an external student of London University.

THE CONSEQUENCES OF UNPLANNED EVENTS

Another important lesson to learn from life is that unanticipated consequences may come out of the most menial of jobs or from unreasonable demands being made on us. We often don't know how one thing can lead to another.

The commander of our camp at RAF, Swanton Morley, was a firm but fair Group Captain. The first time I was marched into his office was in response to weekly standing orders, which he had signed. On this occasion I was assigned to two domestic chores at the same time that were impossible to complete. I explained this to the corporal, who referred it to the sergeant and so on up the chain of command to the station warrant officer. Because the order had been signed by the commanding officer, it was decided that only he could change it, so I was marched in to state my case.

I entered with great trepidation and gave the smartest salute of my career. None of that casual John Wayne stuff! In the RAF, the arm went the longest way up and the shortest way down with a slight quiver of the fingertips. That showed real respect. The commanding officer heard my explanation, thanked me for bringing it up and changed the standing orders.

A few weeks later I received an order to appear before the Group Captain for a second time. I had no idea why. When he stood me at ease, his order—no, it was more of a request—bowled me over. "Gibbs," he said, "I would like you to consider giving an inspirational message to the camp over the loud-speaker system on a Friday night before the monthly Saturday inspection." I wanted the floor to open up, because I knew I could not refuse my commanding officer.

He arranged for me to go to the office where camp announcements were made. I had worked hard preparing what I thought might be a suitable message, but today I have no idea what I said, which is perhaps just as well. I thought I would do it live, but to my horror discovered that it had to be prerecorded (a sensible precaution), which meant that I was with the rest of the guys in my billet doing the spit and polish when the "inspirational" program began. Before my message, a recording by baritone George Beverley Shea was played. Anyone who is a fan of Billy Graham knows that before he spoke, Shea sang. (When I met Shea in 1984 and told him that he had been my lead singer, he enjoyed the story so much that he took off his necktie and gave it to me as a keepsake.)

More than twenty years later I was speaking at a meeting in Guildford when I noticed my former Group Captain in the audience, now long since retired from the RAF. The chairperson hadn't done his homework and apologized that he didn't know the speaker, so he asked me to introduce myself. I said that to one person in the audience I was . . . and then gave my RAF service number, rank and name. He gave me a knowing wink.

LEARNING TO WITNESS WITH HUMILITY, GRACE AND BOLDNESS

I soon learned in the RAF that it's okay to be a person of faith, provided you are for real, you don't think you have all the answers and you recognize that you are answerable to the guys around you. You have to be able to laugh at yourself and not be defensive. The worst thing was a "holier than thou" attitude. Inconsistencies were quickly spotted because we were living together at close quarters 24/7. Thankfully, God had gifted me with a keen sense of humor, though it sometimes got me in trouble. I learned to be friendly with everyone, while choosing my friends carefully.

Although my parents were not churchgoers, they held to high ethical standards. They were faithful to one another; I don't remember any bad language, and my dad hardly every drank, though he was a chain smoker. Eventually my mom banned him from smoking in the house; each of the two downstairs rooms were only nine feet square and quickly filled with cigarette smoke. After that I noticed that he visited the outside toilet more frequently and for longer than usual, and I found the occasional matchstick in the toilet bowl. He also took to sucking mints. Eventually the heavy smoking killed him, causing hardening of the arteries that resulted in an aortic aneurysm.

LEARNING PATIENCE IN ORDER TO BUILD TRUST

One learns in life that God has a way of working through seemingly insurmountable obstacles. It has been said that there are often three stages in any work of God: impossible, possible, accomplished! The mission of God always seems greater than the resources at hand. The Lord often plans it that way so that we rely on him and then give him the glory.

I met my girlfriend, Renee, to whom I became engaged by the time I was twenty, in church in our home city of Nottingham. We saw a lot of each other at Youth Fellowship. Neither of our families had cars, and we didn't have any money to go anywhere. Renee and I were committed to one another by the time I went into the RAF.

I've already mentioned that during my trade training in the RAF, I was given permission to visit a theological college to inquire about future training. The principal (the president) of the college asked me if I had a girlfriend. On learning I did, he asked me what she was doing. She had left school at fifteen, which was common in those days, and was working in a women's clothing store in the city center in the stock room. He said that if I were to train for ministry in the Church of England, I would not be given permission to marry until a year before my ordination, which was six years in the future. Then he invited me to introduce Renee to him in the future.

Renee went to London with me for an interview in which the principal suggested that she consider training for a career that would prepare her for her future life. Becoming either a teacher or a nurse was his suggestion. Both seemed out of reach, because she didn't have the educational qualifications. But her dream was to become a nurse.

Soon after, our pastor's wife was bitten by their dog, which resulted in a short stay in the General Hospital in Nottingham. Each morning the matron (senior nursing officer) did her rounds of the ward, which was as strict as a military inspection. Every item had to be in place; all bed blankets and sheets perfectly straight and with "hospital corners" on every tuck-in. The nurses stood by the beds, and even the patients who were well enough to sit up in bed sat at attention.

During the matron's inspection, she would stop and chat with some of the patients. In conversation with our pastor's wife, the matron bemoaned the fact of a shortage of Christian nurses with a real sense of vocation. "I know someone," replied the pastor's wife. "She has good character but does not have the formal educational training." The matron said that she would like to meet her. So Renee went for an interview, was given a basic educational test in English and math, and to her amazement was accepted into nursing school and would eventually become an RN.

During those difficult six years of waiting, we remained

faithful to each other though we were separated for so much of the time. Neither of us would recommend a long engagement, but it was good that we learned to trust each other. For the past thirty-five years, my work as a missions advocate and then as a college professor and seminar leader has meant frequent absences and trips around the world. It takes a strong woman to keep a passionate young guy on the straight and narrow!

When my grandson's interview with the Air Force recruiting officer came to an end, we drove home, stopping on the way at Starbucks to chat about the experience. We agreed that it had been a good morning in which we had both done our best.

On the journey home, I began to reflect silently on the path my life had taken since my own interview fifty-three years before with the Royal Air Force. At that time I had little clear idea of where my life was leading or whether my dream of becoming a pastor one day was simply an unrealistic expectation. But I had learned so much during those twenty-four months. Officers I respected had encouraged me. Military service had given me opportunities. I had learned to develop good study habits and personal discipline. And I had learned to be self-motivated as I worked alone on my correspondence courses in the educational center and then sat for the qualifying exams.

How Leaders Emerge

For the past twenty-five years, I've been a professor at Fuller Theological Seminary in Pasadena, California—one of the largest seminaries educating and training Christian leaders of many traditions and from around the world. In my master's level classes, I've had a number of students preparing for chaplaincy services in all of the armed forces, and within our doctor of ministry program we have military chaplains earning a higher degree to develop their ministry skills to meet new challenges. Two days before my grandson's interview, I pulled the stats to discover that we have forty-four chaplains who have graduated with their doctor of ministry degrees; fourteen are currently in the program, and twelve are US Air Force chaplains.

During the past ten years, I've become increasingly interested in the emergence and equipping of a new generation of leaders. While doing research for a book, I interviewed many leaders in their thirties as well as some older men and women who realize that our culture has changed, requiring not just younger leaders but leaders with different outlooks and skill sets. The book was eventually published in 2005 as *LeadershipNext*. I discovered in my research that the challenge of leadership development for cultures in rapid transition is not confined to the church but also affects the business world.

The outstanding question was to what extent it affected the military. The chaplains and those students with military experience assured me that many of my observations did, in fact, translate.

I've always kept just one foot in the academic seminary environment and the other among church leaders and laypeople, among whom I've led seminars for many years, often on the topic of leadership in a changing culture. At the end of one session, a gentleman of military bearing (once you've served, you recognize it) introduced himself, and in the course of conversation told me he was a Major General in the US Air Force. I nearly died on the spot. There was I, never having made it to Corporal, presuming to lecture on leadership with a Major General in the room. But he quickly reassured me that my observations and analyses were confirmed by what they were encountering with the young leadership emerging in the service.

Since that time he has become a personal friend and has invited me to share those insights among pastors and lay leaders at several conferences.

DEBRIEFING AT STARBUCKS

My grandson is now serving in the US Air Force. Years ago, the Royal Air Force took me on (they didn't have much choice, unless they failed me on medical grounds) and helped make me what I am today.

As my grandson and I finished our drinks at Starbucks after his initial interview, I realized more than ever before just how significant those two years in the RAF had been in turning around and transforming my life. I pray the same will be true for him.

In the course of reminiscing I've come to realize that the significant turning points in our life together as a married couple and a family often arose out of incidents that seemed insignificant and disconnected at the time. But in the purposes of God, they were decisive.

The other day I read an anonymous quotation with which I can completely identify: "If you want to make God laugh, just tell him your plans." God's guidance is different for each one of us. Some people are driven and inspired throughout life by a single, clear vision. We rejoice with you if this describes your experience. But God has mostly taken Renee and me by surprise, and we have learned that he delights in doing it.

QUESTIONS FOR THOUGHT AND DISCUSSION

1. List the "chapters" in your life. When did the significant turning points occur and what precipitated them?

2. What wrong turns have you taken, and what were the consequences? How did the Lord intervene to get you back on track?

3. As you reflect on the grace of God in your life, what particular things do you want to express gratitude for and celebrate?

PRAXIS

EQUIPPING LEADERS FOR MINISTRY.

God has called us to ministry. But it's not enough to have a vision for ministry if you don't have the practical skills for it. Nor is it enough to do the work of ministry if what you do is headed in the wrong direction. We need both vision *and* expertise for effective ministry. We need *praxis*.

Praxis puts theory into practice. It brings cutting-edge ministry expertise from visionary practitioners. You'll find sound biblical and theological foundations for ministry in the real world, with concrete examples for effective action and pastoral ministry. Praxis books are more than the "how to" – they're also the "why to." And because *being* is every bit as important as *doing*, Praxis attends to the inner life of the leader as well as the outer work of ministry. Feed your soul, and feed your ministry.

If you are called to ministry, you know you can't do it on your own. Let Praxis provide the companions you need to equip God's people for life in the kingdom.

www.ivpress.com/praxis